Sydney's Northern Beaches

Sydney's Northern Beaches

David Messent

This book is for everyone who lives on or visits Sydney's Northern Beaches

Published by
David Messent Photography
Sydney
First edition published 1999

Photography and design   David Messent
Helicopter flights   Helicopter Charter
Typesetting and map   Max Peatman

Printed in Singapore by Kyodo

Previous page: Sand ripples and reflections, Narrabeen Lakes.

Contents

Manly

Manly and the Northern Beaches. A jetcat is just approaching Manly Wharf.

Manly

Looking south towards Manly from Queenscliff Beach.

In 1923 the Manly Daily invited readers to enter a competition for the words of a song on Manly titled 'Manly by the Sea'. The following verses are an abbreviation of a song by Mr Bailey, entered under the nom de plume of 'Cynthia'.

> The wind blows in the old pine trees
> Sweet scent from tropic isles
> And fanned by each caressing breeze
> The lazy ocean smiles…
>
> The Corso's all agleam with light,
> It's magic calls to me.
> For tis a land of dear delight,
> Sweet Manly by the Sea…
>
> From Queenscliff to the Fairy Bower
> They walk in ecstasy!
> For this is love's own witching hour
> At Manly by the sea.

Manly has a timeless quality about it. Somehow one imagines The Corso, the pines and the promenades have always been there, but they are relatively new. Indeed Manly was virtually uninhabited for the first 60 years of white settlement even though Governor Phillip discovered and graced the peninsula with a name before discovering and naming Sydney Cove.

Early discovery

Phillip set out to explore Sydney Harbour from Botany Bay and spent the first night at Camp Cove. Later the following day, as he related in a despatch to Lord Sydney:

> The boats, in passing near a point of land in the harbour, were seen by a number of men, and twenty of them waded into the water unarmed, received what was offered them, and examined the boats with a curiosity that gave me a much higher opinion of them… and their confidence and manly behaviour made me give the name of Manly Cove to this place.

Phillip doesn't mention in his despatch the date he was first at Manly, but the time is confirmed by a journal entry by William Bradley, a cartographer with the First Fleet. Bradley, in his diary on 29th January 1788, mentioned taking part in a survey with Captain Hunter. The party rowed to Manly, and:

> As we were going into the first cove on the east side, called Spring Cove, we were joined by three canoes, with one man in each…
>
> We were soon joined by a dozen of them and found three among them with trinkets, etc. hanging about them that had been given to them a week before by the Governor on his first visit to this place.

Thus Phillip was there a week before, on the 21st or 22nd. Sydney was named on the 26th.

First land grants

Manly remained a camping ground for a local Aboriginal tribe until 1st January 1810, when Macquarie, on his first day as Governor, granted 'Unto Richard Cheers, his Heirs and Assigns to have and to hold for ever 100 acres of land…

lying in the district of North Harbour.' Cheers, a convict, received the grant as a reward for heroic conduct in helping to save the convict transport *Guardian* which was nearly wrecked off Cape Town. The land, which extended from the Harbour to the Ocean Beach in the vicinity of Ashburner Street and up the slope towards North Head, was granted with the stipulation that 20 acres were to be cultivated and that no land was to be sold for five years. Cheers brought with him to live at Manly his convict wife Margaret Foggarty, though she died not long after on 23rd August 1810, the jurors at the subsequent inquest coming to the unanimous conclusion that she 'came to her death in consequence of excessive inebriety'. Cheers established an orchard on his grant and the holding became known as 'Cheer's Farm.' The same day that Cheers received his grant Macquarie also granted 30 acres at Manly to Gilbert Baker.

D'Arcy Wentworth acquired Cheers' estate in 1818 and due to restrictions imposed by his will, most of it remained bush until the 1880s. The same was true for many years of the rest of Manly. In 1822 there were only two families resident there and by 1841, according to the official census, there were 25 people living in four houses at Manly. There was also a house at the Quarantine Station, one at Middle Harbour, two at North Harbour (Balgowlah), a house at Dee Why and a house at Long Reef. The situation in 1848, according to Wells Geographical Dictionary of the Australian Colonies was that 'The Parish of Manly Cove, comprising all the land between North Head and Narrabeen Lagoon, contains 24 houses and 63 inhabitants.' So Manly was just bush and sandhills with a few scattered houses and farms when in 1853 Henry Gilbert Smith 'The father of Manly' took an interest in the district.

The rocky landscape on the ocean side of Shelly Beach.

Henry Gilbert Smith

Smith thought Manly was like a dream come true, later describing it to a friend:

> It's situation – seven or eight miles by water from Sydney, is as fine a thing as you can imagine and it takes in the only ground which has the sea beach on one side and a fine sandy cove on the other. There is no place to equal it for beauty. It is truly delightful. There is nothing like it in the wide, wide world…

'Gentleman Smith' as he was known by the locals, was a native of Northamptonshire, England, who emigrated to Australia and became a successful merchant and land speculator. In May 1853 Smith bought 20 acres of land in Manly for £8 an acre including some rising ground on the hill west of the Harbour Beach which he called 'Fairlight' after a village near Hastings. The following year Smith built 'Fairlight House' on the hill and completed a 50 foot jetty on Manly Cove as a berth for a 23 ton wooden paddle steamer *The Brothers*, Manly's first ferry.

Smith bought up more land in Manly (his holdings eventually amounted to 120 acres) and boldly set about turning the peninsula into a Brighton of the antipodes. When he drew his first street plan in January 1855 he had the then raging Crimean War in the back of his mind because present day Sydney Road was pencilled in as 'Sebastopol Street', parallel to it to the north was 'Raglan Street' (which survives), the sandstone boulders at the top of the ridge were called 'The Rocks of Sebastopol' and below them was 'Alma Crescent'. Whistler Street was named as a token of affection for his nephew, Thomas Whistler Smith. Opposite the ferry wharf Smith built the Italianate Pier Hotel, cut a track through the bush to the Ocean Beach he called 'The Corso' after a street in Rome, and by the addition of a public 'pleasure garden', fun fair, refreshment tents and a maze had turned Manly into a resort 60 years before Bondi became popular.

Manly jetcat.

The ferry passes Sydney Harbour Bridge on her way to Manly.

In June 1855 Smith wrote to his brother in England:

> The amusement I derive in making my improvements at Manly is, no doubt, the cause of my greater enjoyment, in fact I never feel a dull day while there. I should long ere this have been with you if it had not been for this hobby of mine, in thinking I am doing good in forming a village or watering place for the inhabitants of Sydney.

And recounted his latest endeavours in October 1856:

> a building for warm baths is now in progress and many other improvements in the way of walks and clearing out the bush. The place is really so very beautiful I have no fear of its progress. I spend at least five days there in every week.

Smith's walks were cut through the bush to elevated spots above Manly, one of which he called Eagle's Nest where he built a wooden viewing platform. As an added attraction on one of the walks he contracted a stone mason to sculpt a stone kangaroo. It still exists, though now heavily weathered, overlooking the ocean on Kangaroo Street. Land 100 feet from high water mark on the Harbour and Ocean Beach was reserved for public space. The road next to the promenade on the ocean side Smith called 'The Steyne' after a street in Brighton. Not long after Smith built the Steyne Hotel overlooking the ocean at the end of The Corso.

To ensure the settlement's future prosperity Smith built 'a little rustic church', providing £50 a year for the salary of the clergyman, and donated the land for two other churches, a schoolhouse (which opened in 1858 with 19 pupils), a police station and a 'School of Arts'. Smith's aforementioned 'warm baths' (a public bath-house on East Esplanade), was converted to the Manly Art Gallery in 1930.

In 1880 Smith sold Fairlight House and soon after returned to England. He was a widower, having outlived his first two Australian wives, but at the age of nearly 80 he married for the third time an Irish girl and spent his last days with her at Hove, Brighton, where he died aged 84 on 1st April, 1886. Most of Manly's present day parks and waterside reserves were left to the people of Manly in Smith's will, including North Steyne, East and West Esplanade, Kangaroo Park and Ivanhoe Park.

Early memories

A record of life in Manly's early days was left by George Aurousseau, the son of a Frenchman from Bourges and an English mother who spent his childhood in Manly from the age of four in 1868. Aurousseau wrote his memoirs when he was 88, to 'leave a record of my memories of Old Manly whilst I still have the faculties to do so.' His father bought a bakery business on the north side of The Corso and later purchased the premises and land from Henry Gilbert Smith. Aurousseau recalled:

> We had no water service or sewerage in those days and many an hour I had to spend pumping up tubs of water for the needs of the business and for an occasional bath... as pump water was very hard, we had to buy rain water for clothes wash. The only sanitation was earth closets, deep pits in the sand.

At that time the land north of The Corso was 'gum trees and scrub... nearly all the way to the lagoon, with a few scattered houses.' While on the south side at the present day corner of South Steyne and Ashburner Street 'Mr Smith had a small dairy and used to sell milk to the residents (and nearby) a pretty little creek of fresh water emptied into the ocean...'. On the opposite side of The Corso from the bakery were 'many large Banksia trees... which when in flower attracted large numbers of gilbirds and mockers and my brother used to cross The Corso with his gun... and soon shoot a fine lot of birds from which my father would

Manly ferry approaching Manly Wharf.

Manly jetcat leaves a trail of white spray in her wake as she departs Manly Wharf for Sydney.

Enjoying a Sunday stroll on the promenade at Manly Beach.

prepare a very delectable dish.' On the heights west of the village 'There was a big flock of goats which used to live among (the rocks)... There was a fine big Billy who bossed the flock and chased us when we got too near.'

If the weather was stormy and the ferries had been taken off because of the swell running through the Heads, George would 'walk from Manly to the Spit where I was rowed across by one of the Ellerys who ran the punt service. From here I walked to Lavender Bay, crossed in the ferry to Circular Quay, took a horse bus at Macquarie Place to Tooth's Brewery, bought a can of yeast', then, as often as not soaked to the skin, Aurousseau returned the same way to Manly, because as his father's bakery was the only one in Manly, if there was no yeast, there was no bread for the people of Manly. 'There was no house from Manly to Ellery's stone house on the hill above the Spit and I have been at such times the only human being all the way.'

The Manly ferries

Manly was effectively an island cut off from Sydney because the only way to get there except for undertaking an arduous journey overland was by ferry. The ferries were the key to Manly's success and it was the creation of the ferry service that brought Smith's dream of turning Manly into a resort a reality. The *Empire* newspaper of 25th May 1859 reported that 'between 12,000 and 13,000 persons visited the beautiful indentation on Sydney Harbour known as Manly Beach' and they all travelled by ferry.

Early ferries were graced with titles such as *The Huntress*, the *Planet*, the *Phantom*, the *Mystery*, the *Irresistable* and the *Brightside*. The *Phantom* was famous for the perfect smoke rings she blew from her tall smoke stack as she got underway, and as the venue for the hot potato club. During the 1860s if enough Manly residents were going into Sydney for a night out they would charter the *Phantom* and arrive in Sydney at 7.30 p.m. There was no shelter at Circular Quay and the ferry departed for Manly at 11 o'clock, so it was the duty of early arrivals to procure potatoes and take them on board to roast on the engine furnace coals for the rest of the passengers to munch on the hour long return trip.

But although a significant portion of Sydney's population came to visit Manly on holidays, it wasn't a place where they immediately flocked to live. In 1856 the population was still only 73, and it wasn't until 1871 that it rose to 500. But it was that first glimpse of Manly's charms after a trip on the ferry, arriving at the Harbour Beach, then strolling through The Corso to the Ocean Beach, that convinced visitors that here was a place where they should permanently reside. In 1888 the population from Manly to Narrabeen Lagoon reached 2,000. In the 1890s when two rival ferry companies were vying for business and the fare came down to 3d return (in 1854 it was a shilling each way) enormous numbers of day-trippers started to flock to the Village. This was in spite of the fact that visitors weren't allowed to swim during the day and if they wanted to cool off had to be content with a paddle.

Daylight swimming

An 1838 Act of Parliament forbade all public swimming in Manly except between the hours of 8 p.m. and 6 a.m. This situation prevailed into the 20th century, when, according to Percy Gledhill:

> On a hot day in September, 1902, some yachting lads, gaily attired, took a joyous plunge into the cool Pacific. But much to their dismay, upon coming out they were all arrested and taken to the local lock-up.

Mr W. H. Gocher, Editor and Proprietor of the 'Manly and North Sydney News,' questioned the police about the matter… (and) told them they would have to arrest him on the following Sunday, as he meant to test what he described as an absurdity and injustice. In the next issue of his paper he proclaimed his intention 'of bounding in for a bathe on the morrow' and the Police would therefore be expected to do their duty and arrest him.

The time arrived and he entered the breakers and to use his own words 'It was the most enjoyable bathe of my life-time.' However nothing exciting happened as there were very few people about, notwithstanding his press bragging.

No posse of police came flying down with drawn swords to the water's edge to bring him forth and arrest him…

On the following Tuesday night, at the Council meeting, Mr Gocher's action was discussed and the Mayor… stated that before he would tolerate all-day bathing he would pull down all the (bathing) sheds…

Mr Gocher again announced his intention of once more going in for a bathe at the same time and in the same place. The day came, he went, in but nothing eventful happened except that a few people strolled up to watch events. He decided to try a third time when matters started to get merrier.

The law swooped down on him and he was arrested and bailed out by Frank Donovan.

He then interviewed Mr Fosbery, Inspector General of Police, who received him kindly.

To quote Mr Gocher – 'I felt sure he had been well posted regarding the happenings at Manly.' He said that no magistrate would convict me, but that men would have to wear neck-to-knee costumes…

(Following further campaigning) At the meeting of the Council held on the 9th March 1903, a letter of Mr Gocher's was discussed asking for better accommodation for bathers on the Ocean Beach. At the same meeting the Council decided to provide flags to mark the danger spots and also that the Manly Life Saving Society be asked to fix flags morning and evening…

A motion was passed (by Council) on 2nd November, 1903, that the By Law prohibiting bathing after 7 a.m. be rescinded. This was adopted, In lieu therof another By Law was passed allowing all day bathing on the condition that every one over the age of eight years was clad in a neck-to-knee costume. The penalty for offenders was fixed at not more than £1 and not less than five shillings.

This sort of thing doesn't happen very often. The Manly ferry aground on Manly Cove Beach.

The law was enforced, though as time went on not very seriously. On 22nd October 1936 a man was fined one shilling in Manly Court for being 'nude to the waist' on the Beach.

Gocher's friends presented him with a purse of fifty sovereigns and a watch which included the inscription, 'W. H. Gocher Esq. Pioneer of all day surf bathing… Entered the water 2nd October 1902.'

Once daylight bathing was allowed in 1903, the Sly brothers started Australia's first Life Saving Service at Manly, operating from an old fishing boat. But inevitably there were tragedies. At first swimming was segregated, males at one part of the beach, females at another, but after two women were drowned, the next day, according to Vialoux:

the women bathers… gathered near the men for their own protection, some of them joining the male community, and talking over the tragedy of the day before. Then a wave of common sense swept the whole local surfbathing fraternity; the barriers of sex magically disappeared. The next Sunday found all the surfers, men and women, boys and girls, bathing together, feeling safe and happy.

Manly's heyday

In 1922 the population of Manly reached 17,000. At that time three fifths of householders at Manly had been there originally for a holiday and then decided

Queenscliff Surf Club.

to come back to live. 'They came, they saw, and Manly conquered' is how Vialoux put it.

An 'expert' writing in the 1920s and cheerfully disregarding the presence of the Quarantine Station on the hill believed it was the healthy aspect of Manly that was its main attraction, located on the coast which usually made it at least five degrees cooler than Sydney and:

> Surrounded on three sides by the sea, it is, like Venice, free from dust, and dust is the carrier of germs and microbes… The Manlyite… returns to his home knowing that strongly as the sea-breezes may blow, they bring with them no choking dirt or malignant atoms…

To cater for the increase in traffic, big fast streamlined ferries were laid down in the United Kingdom and with their windows boarded up steamed out to Australia. They included the 498 ton *Baragoola*, seating 1523 passengers, (in service for 61 years from 1922 and at time of writing rusting away at a wharf in Balmain) the 799 ton sister ships *Curl Curl* and *Dee Why* (on the run from 1928 to the 1960s then both scuttled off Sydney) and the 1203 ton *SS South Steyne* seating 1781, reputed to be the largest all passenger steam ferry in the world (operational from 1938 to 1974 and at time of writing a floating restaurant at Darling Harbour). The 1930s were the bleak years of the depression but they were Manly's heyday, for everyone could still afford a few pence for the ferry fare and the tremendous crowds that flocked to Manly's beaches were double what they ever are today. The record was set on 27th January 1936 when over 100,000 passengers travelled to Manly by ferry.

A trip by ferry for the first time is a great thrill, and even for those who live in Manly and commute by ferry every day to Sydney the journey still holds a special place in their hearts. Sir Roden Cutler, appointed Governor of N.S.W. in 1966, was born and spent the early years of his life in Manly. He wrote in his introduction to a book on Manly, 'The Harbour and the ferry trip gave us time to think before we began the working day in the city, and time to unwind on our return in the evening.' Cutler, with the other regulars on the run, used to place bets on the number of seagulls which would be perching on the pillar at Bradley's Head.

Ferry dramas

But the trip wasn't without its dramas. In the early days the engine of the ferry *Manly* expired while the ship was in a heavy swell between the Heads, and was only saved from being dashed onto the rocks near the Quarantine Station after a line was thrown from the *Brighton*.

In 1934 the *Baragoola* collided with a whale off North Head. The unfortunate creature was seen swimming away, but was mortally wounded, and its rotting carcass surfaced three days later. It was towed out to sea by the fire tug *Pluvius* followed by hundreds of cawing seagulls but drifted back again, first to South Head, then to Botany Bay. Finally a tug towed it far out over the horizon and it was never heard of again. A more embarrassing incident befell the captain of the *Dee Why*. After leaving Manly Wharf on Christmas night 1946 she steamed into a freak fog at 10 p.m. and was hard aground on Georges Head fifteen minutes later. Her 700 passengers were taken off by two other ferries. She was refloated, rudderless, next morning.

Usually the ferry stops at the wharf, but occasionally something goes wrong, even on the modern ferries. At 9 a.m. on 10th March 1983, the recently launched *Freshwater* was berthing at Manly Wharf, when the ship's computer engaged

The crescent of Manly Beach seen from Queenscliff.

North Steyne Surf Club.

Riding the breakers at Queenscliff.

Marching drill with a lifeline during a surf carnival at Manly.

the propellor, sending the ship through the swimming enclosure net and onto Manly Cove Beach. She was refloated on the high tide at 3 p.m. with the assistance of a tug.

The Corso

On arrival by ferry in Manly on a busy Sunday you're swept along by a tide of humanity which carries you across the road and along The Corso to the Ocean Beach. The writer D.H. Lawrence came this way in May 1922 and stopped with his wife for a cup of tea. He thought Manly was 'Like a bit of Margate with seaside shops and restaurants, till you come out on a promenade at the end; and there is the wide Pacific rolling in on the yellow sand…'. One of the first things you pass on The Corso on the way to the beach is Manly War Memorial, unveiled during the Great War in October 1916. The memorial was given to the citizens of Manly by Mark Mitchell, whose son, Allen David Mitchell was the first soldier from Manly to fall in the conflict.

At the corner of The Corso overlooking the Pacific is The Steyne Hotel. On the evening of Empire Day, 24th May 1906, members of the Manly Brass Band were enjoying a drink at The Steyne after a concert on The Corso when they were told that the French barque *Vincennes* had run aground on Manly Beach. The band members dashed with their instruments onto the sand and played the Marseillaise in honour of the Gallic crew. The barque was succesfully refloated a few days later. The band went on to great things, winning the Australian Championship in 1911.

Though The Corso has been the main street of Manly since the 1850s when

Looking towards Queenscliff from the south end of Manly Beach. Lifesavers patrol the area between the flags.

Surf carnival at Manly. These days the hand rowed life-saving boats are mostly used only in competition. Beach patrols are carried out by inflatable 'rubber duckies'.

All eyes are on the boats when a race is underway.

Sydney's Northern Beaches

Norfolk Island pines on the Ocean promenade.

Pines also line the Esplanade on the Harbour side of Manly.

Henry Gilbert Smith laid narrow planks on top of the sand to make for easier walking and built a small bridge to cross the swamp that was then in the vicinity of Whistler Street, there were those who once felt another street laid better to the title. Broad Victoria Parade with its avenue of Norfolk Island Pines running parrallel one street to the east, was laid out by the developers of the Bassett-Darley estate in the 1880s in the hope that it would become the pre-eminent street in Manly eclipsing the narrower Corso. They even attempted to have the ferry wharf moved to a site at the Harbour end of the Parade. However it wasn't to be.

Manly's pines

Entering onto the promenade next to the Ocean Beach, you are greeted by the sight of Manly's Norfolk Island pines. The pines are as much a part of Manly as the Opera House is a part of Sydney. They are not native to Manly, the first ones were planted by Henry Gilbert Smith at Fairlight House and on the Harbour foreshore nearby. In 1877 the first Mayor of Manly, Thomas Rowe, instituted a Tree Planting Beautification Scheme for Manly. Rowe, a prospector, architect, Commander of the Engineers in the army, and father of 16 children, found time among his other duties to take the fledgeling Municipality under his wing. He planted Moreton Bay figs in strategic locations such as the parks on East Esplanade and next to Belgrave Street (they still exist and are now veritable giants) and started plantings of Norfolk Island pines on the reserves next to the Harbour and Ocean Beaches. The young trees were brought from Norfolk Island 50 or 100 at a time and fertilised by seaweed gathered on the beach and dug into the sand. Early plantings were not very successful and a base of soil and leaf mould was found to give the seedlings a better chance. Rowe's work was carried on by subsequent mayors, and by the late nineteenth century pines were planted in a double crescent along the entire length of the Harbour and Ocean Beaches.

During the war the defence command issued an order to cut down all the pines on the Ocean Beach to provide a clear field of fire for defending artillery in case of invasion. Preparations were put in place and one pine was cut down at South Steyne near the surf club before common sense prevailed and the order was lifted. A plaque on the stump was a reminder to passers by of how Manly nearly lost its pines. A more recent and devastating threat to the pines has been the presence in the sea water of detergents from household waste entering the ocean. Onshore winds deposit small quantities of detergent on the pine needles of the trees, stripping off their natural protective oils and killing them. This was particularly the case at the north end of the Beach where the trees all but disappeared. A vigorous replanting scheme has since been instituted, and household waste is now pumped further out to sea, so it shouldn't be too long before Manly's pines regain their former glory.

Seaside walks

On the promenade near The Steyne Hotel is Manly Visitor's Information Bureau, where the friendly staff offer plenty of free information on what to see and do in the district. From Manly Surf Club at the south end of the beach its a ten minute walk to Shelly Beach. The path passes a cafe on the corner of Bower Lane. This spot is known as Fairy Bower. In days gone by there was a substantial beach here backed by a grassy reserve, and old photos show crowds of bathers enjoying the surf and families of daytrippers sitting on the grass basking in the sun. But a storm swept away the sand and the reserve has since been developed for housing. In the mid-nineteenth century when the area was still a tranquil setting of flowers and ferns like a 'fairyland' it was a popular place for picnics and church outings from Manly.

Shelly Beach, comprised of millions of finely ground sea shells, is one of only two west facing beaches on the east coast of Australia. From the north end of the beach a track leads around the headland, across the carpark at the top and up some steps cut in the rock to a high lookout with a bird's eye view of Shelly Beach and Manly.

North Head

From Manly town centre, the long straight hill of Darley Road leads through Manly's suburban houses, past Manly Hospital, to North Head Scenic Drive, which continues for two kilometres through bushland to a car park on the headland. On the way, just past Manly Hospital, the road passes beneath a sandstone archway. This is the original entrance to Manly Quarantine Station. When the Station was in use the way was barred by locked gates and a guard checked vehicles entering and leaving.

From the carpark at North Head a circular walking track about a kilometre long winds through the heathland on the Head past one or two concrete observation posts constructed during the Second World War. The track leads to a series of lookouts on the south side of the Head with views across the mouth of the Harbour to South Head and straight down the Harbour to the city. North Head is the highest and the most spectacular lookout of all the reserves on the Harbour foreshores, and provides a good vantage point for viewing the entry to Sydney of the world's great ocean liners and naval ships.

Leaving the car park at North Head, two hundred metres on the right North Fort Road leads to the National Artillery Museum. The Museum has comprehensive displays of armaments from the First and Second World Wars, and examples of ordnance from more modern conflicts, including an Iraqi gun captured during the Gulf War. A tour of the Museum includes a walk through the tunnels built to link

The clock on Manly Corso.

Manly Corso spans the sandspit between the Harbour and Ocean Beaches.

White houses with tiled roofs overlooking Manly Lagoon resemble a scene from Provence.

the big coastal defence guns placed on the headland during the 1930s. Unfortunately, the guns themselves were removed during the 1960s. Rottnest Island off Perth still has its identical guns in place, but so far requests by the National Artillery Museum for a 'loan' of one of them has fallen on deaf ears.

Manly Quarantine Station

On the way back to Manly, at the point where North Head Scenic Drive makes a sharp turn to the right, on the left a road leads to Manly Quarantine Station. Daytime tours or a nightime 'ghost tour' can be arranged through the New South Wales National Parks and Wildlife Service. There are no parking facilities at the Station entrance, so tours start by bus at the terminal at Manly Wharf.

About 60 buildings remain at the Quarantine Station out of the 90 or so that used to occupy the site, most of them dating from the 1870s to the 1920s when the Station saw its heaviest use.

The Station was first set aside as quarantine area in 1828, when the *Bussorah Merchant* arrived in Sydney carrying smallpox. The convicts and their guards were unloaded at Store Beach with some tents and provisions where they were left to fend for themselves for a few weeks, while the crew and some free settlers were confined on board while the ship was moored in Neutral Bay.

The time taken on the journey by sea to Sydney was longer than the incubation period of all known infectious diseases, including typhus, scarlet fever, smallpox and influenza. If a ship carried disease it broke out on board, so judicious quarantine procedures by the authorities prevented epidemics carrying to the Australian mainland. Facilities were expanded to keep pace with the passenger carrying capacity of ocean liners, so that by 1915 the Station could comfortably accommodate over 1,500 souls.

On arrival at the Station jetty, passengers showered in a diluted phenol solution, then dressed in clothes they had previously selected for treatment that had been sterilised in the station's steam rooms or 'autoclaves'. Some passengers who may have been in contact with disease carriers went through a horrifying (and as it was later discovered completely useless) procedure of being shut in a room for ten minutes to inhale zinc sulphate gas in an attempt to kill evil 'miasmas' that may linger in their lungs.

Shipping companies bringing a vessel to Sydney carrying disease were deemed responsible for any quarantine costs incurred on arrival in port, and not only paid the expenses of the station, but housed passengers in a similar style to that they'd enjoyed on board ship, waited on by the ship's crew who also cooked their meals and washed their clothes in a giant brass washing machine powered by a steam engine. Areas of the station were separated into First, Second, Third and 'Asiatic' class accommodation, each with their own restaurants, lounges and sleeping quarters. Passengers fortunate enough not to be carrying disease themselves made the most of their enforced detention, playing cricket or tennis, swimming on Store Beach, wandering the bushland of North Head or walking to an unusual rock formation on the cliff called 'Old Man's Hat' to pose for a picture. Others set to work carving mementoes of their stay on the numerous sandstone rocks above the beaches or in the surrounding bush. There are hundreds of these carvings, over a thousand have been documented and many hundreds more lie uncatalogued on rocks now overgrown by bushland. Some are little more than scratchings on the rock, others look very professional and were executed by stonemasons who travelled out as immigrants. They are the most

Queenscliff Beach.

Queenscliff Rockpool. An early morning swimmer once found they had a shark for company, washed in by a storm the previous night.

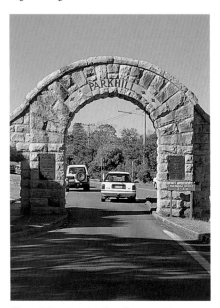

The old entry to the Quarantine Station spans Darley Road on the drive to North Head.

poignant reminder of life on the station and range from sad epitaphs written by relatives for loved ones lost on the voyage out, to jolly tales of living conditions at the Station. There's a memorial to the *William Rodger*, which arrived in 1838, losing 16 to disease on the voyage out and a further 29 at the Station. William Usherwood inscribed his thoughts on stone in 1853, lamenting 'Oh misery of miseries, surely Job can never have been in quarantine.' A message on a rock next to the 'Asiatic quarters' has been translated from Chinese, and reads in part, '…I can only weep sadly to the moon, separated from my parents by vast oceans, whose love I have not reciprocated until this day', while a sailor inscribed in 1935, 'Oh to be in quarantine, now that summer's here, phoning up your friends at work, sending out for beer. Bathe by day and bridge by night, life of endless play. Oh to be in quarantine, banking up your pay.'

The Station was in only occasional use after the 1930s. During the Second World War British evacuee children were temporarily housed there on arrival and the Station was used as a billet for soldiers. The Station's final call to fame was in 1974 when 750 residents from Darwin were temporarily housed there after Cyclone Tracy devastated the town on Christmas Day. Ten years later in 1984, the Station was closed completely for quarantine purposes, and assumed its present status as a historic site, run by the National Parks and Wildlife Service.

A tour of the Station today around the deserted buildings with their wide shady verandahs, evokes a strange feeling of a land that time has passed by. The old sleeping quarters, dining rooms and lounges built at the turn of the century are furnished in the style of the early 1950s, dating to the time the Commonwealth Government last refurbished the Station. Hospital beds from the same era stand neatly against the walls in the Quarantine Station Hospital as if the patients have just left them, and in the morgue medical glass jars and test-tubes line the shelves as if in wait for the ministrations of the pathologists. On a more cheerful note, if you keep your eyes open you may stumble across a treasure trove. Not so long ago a worker looking for white ants under one of the buildings discovered a cache of 50 gold sovereigns, and there's still rumoured to be another hoard hidden by an unfortunate immigrant who couldn't retrieve it before going to the Great Quarantine Station in the sky.

Collins Beach and Store Beach

Leaving the Quarantine Station, continue on North Head Scenic Drive passing on the right the old North Head Army Barracks and School of Artillery. After a few hundred metres turn left into Collins Beach Road, which winds down through a dense pocket of bushland to the Australian Police College. From a parking place on the right just before the College, a path leads through the bush to Collins Beach. Collins Beach, named after Captain David Collins, Judge Advocate with the First Fleet, is a lovely quiet beach surrounded by natural bushland, the peaceful setting enhanced by the sound of a small waterfall cascading over rocks at the southern end. The scene is no doubt little different today to the appearance of the Beach on 7th September 1790 when Phillip met the Aborigine, Bennelong here after receiving from him a gift of meat from a dead whale. Bennelong was an Aborigine who Phillip had captured earlier at Manly, and brought back to Sydney to live with him at Government House. He had recently escaped and made his way back to Manly. As Captain Watkin Tench of the marines tells the story, on meeting Bennelong, Phillip offered him a glass of wine:

> which the other drank off with his former marks of relish and good humour, giving for a toast, as he had been taught, 'the King…'.

The view towards Manly from the lookout above Shelly Beach.

A walking track skirts Shelly Beach Park on the headland.

Holiday crowd at Shelly Beach.

Wind sculpted rocks on North Head.

Matters had proceeded in this friendly train for more than half an hour, when a native, with a spear in his hand, came forward...

The nearer the Governor approached, the greater became the terror and agitation of the Indian. To remove fear, Governor Phillip threw down a (dagger), which he wore at his side. The other, alarmed at the rattle of the (dagger) and probably misconstruing the action, instantly fixed his lance in his throwing stick... the Indian, stepping back with one foot, aimed the lance with such force and dexterity, that striking the Governor's right shoulder just above the collar-bone, the point glancing downward came out at the back, having made a wound of many inches long. The man was observed to keep his eye steadily fixed on the lance until it struck its object when he directly dashed into the woods and was seen no more.

Tench recorded that 'His Excellency described the shock to me as similar to a violent blow, with such energy was the weapon thrown'. Captain John Hunter continued the story:

The Governor... attempted to run towards the boat, holding up the spear with both hands to keep it off the ground, but owing to its great length, the end frequently took the ground and stopped him. Governor Phillip, in this situation, desired Mr Waterhouse to endeavour, if possible, to take the spear out, which he immediately attempted, but observing it to be barbed and the barb quite through, he saw it would be impossible to draw it out. He therefore endeavoured to break it but could not.

While he was making this attempt, another spear was thrown out of the wood and took off the skin between Mr Waterhouse's fore-finger and thumb, which alarmed him a good deal, and he thinks added power to his exertions, for the next attempt he broke it off...

The whole party got down to the boat without any further accident and in two hours they arrived at the government house, when the surgeons were sent for. Mr Balmain, who was the first that arrived, after examining the wound, made everybody happy by assuring them he did not apprehend any fatal consequences from it. He extracted the point of the spear and dressed the wound, and in six weeks the Governor was perfectly recovered.

Phillip insisted his men were not to take any retaliatory action against the offending Aborigine.

From the south end of Collins Beach it's a ten minute clamber over the rocks at low tide to Store Beach. The beach was named after the stores left there for the early inmates of the Quarantine Station.

A track at the north end of Collins Beach leads after five minutes walk to Stuart Street, where there's a park at Little Manly Point on the old gasworks site and a sandy beach at Little Manly Cove.

St Patrick's

However, continuing our journey back towards Manly on Darley Road, we pass on the right the ornate wrought iron gates of St Patrick's seminary. During the nineteenth century over a period of eight years the Catholic church made several requests to the Government for a grant of land on which to build a seminary. Requests for land at Camperdown, Coogee and Cabarita were made and refused, until finally, in July 1863, Governor Bourke agreed to an application for a site in Manly. Many thought the 53 acres offered were granted out of spite, on land which the Governor thought no one would ever need, next to the unsanitary Quarantine Station and the only means of communication with Sydney by boat. In fact the church had received one of the superlative sights in Sydney, on the hill high above Manly with a view along the Northern Beaches, and in 1885 they commenced construction of a college modelled on Maynooth, the national seminary of Ireland. Stone for building was quarried at the Quarantine Station,

North Head guards the entrance to Sydney Harbour.

Early morning scene at the rocks of Shelly Beach Park.

Manly Quarantine Station and Beach.

but an outbreak of smallpox led to the quarry being quarantined, delaying the work for some time.

Ever since it opened in January 1889 the college, perched on the hill above Manly like a medieval castle, has been one of the grandest examples of architecture in Sydney. The interior matches the grace of the outside, with cedar ceilings, doors, door frames and skirtings, and floors and corridors paved with a chequered pattern of black and white marble tiles. The so-called 'Cardinal's Palace', home of the Roman Catholic cardinals in Sydney, was built nearby. In those days when the only access was by sea, St Patrick's and the Cardinals Palace were on the same block of land, it was only later that they were separated by Darley Road. The Cardinals now reside in Sydney in a dwelling next to St Mary's Cathedral and the 'Palace' is part of St Paul's Christian Brothers School.

The writer Thomas Keneally, author of 'Schindler's Ark', who later lived on the Northern Beaches at Avalon then Bilgola, studied at St Patrick's for the Roman Catholic Priesthood, but left before ordination in 1960. While on the subject of authors, in 1902 Henry Lawson lived close by at 15 Darley Road. The seminary now houses the International College of Tourism and Hotel Management.

St Andrew's Church

Just past St Patrick's Darley Road turns to the right and there's a beautiful view of Manly to greet you from the top of the hill. It's a good spot to loiter for a moment at sunrise, and watch the sun's rays caress the houses on the hill above the village then cascade down the terraces of streets to the beach. One of the first structures to be bathed with light is the stone tower of St Andrew's Presbyterian Church on Raglan Street. But the view of Manly and the Church from Darley Road was one that the Reverend J. Anderson Gardiner, 2nd minister of the Church from 1895-1914, never saw. He was blind. A memorial plaque to the Reverand in the Church closes with the passage 'He endured as seeing Him who is invisible.'

St Andrew's was designed by John Sulman (later Sir John Sulman, after whom the famous architectural prize is named) in a unique Romanesque style. When the church was opened in April 1890 the design received world-wide acclaim and was featured in the Building and Engineering Journal of 5th November 1892. The floor has a gentle slope towards the pulpit to ensure every member of the congregation has a good view. Hanging on the wall inside the Church is a painting by Tom Roberts of Miss Bryant, who for 60 years was the church organist.

St Andrew's stands on a prominent site on the hill overlooking Ivanhoe Park and Manly Oval. In 1897 the oval was the venue for a cricket match between Lord Sheffield's eleven led by the great W.G. Grace and the 'Men-of-Manly' team. Although the visitors won, the match was not one of Grace's more remarkable performances, he only scored 35 and 4 in the two innings.

These days we tend to take Ivanhoe Park with its sports ground, bowling ground and tennis courts for granted, but we must thank its presence to the foresight of an early Mayor of Manly, Mr Hayes. When the site, which included a stone quarry, was sold in the 1880s, Hayes bought it with his own money to save it from development, then later sold it at cost to the State after persuading the Premier to buy it for the people of Manly.

The walk to The Spit

Manly Wharf is the starting point for one of the best harbourside walks in Sydney, following the shoreline for nine kilometres to The Spit Bridge. From the west

Quiet sheltered beaches line Spring Cove.

Collins Beach was the scene of a famous encounter between Governor Phillip and an Aborigine.

The easiest way to reach Store Beach is by boat.

The Cardinal's Palace.

side of Manly Wharf, follow the promenade along Manly Cove Beach past the netted off swimming pool. At the east end of the Beach are Manly Art Gallery and Museum and Oceanworld Aquarium. The Art Gallery, housed in Gilbert Smith's former Public Baths, has a significant collection, including a Rubens and one of Tom Roberts' most celebrated works 'The Flower Sellers'.

Fairlight Beach

The path continues on a well-maintained walkway as it winds and undulates through the pine trees past Delwood and Fairlight Beach. Next to the path is the site of Gilbert Smith's 'Fairlight House'. The house itself was demolished to make way for a block of flats in 1939 and all that remains are remnants of the garden, a stone wall, and three Norfolk Island pines.

North Harbour Reserve, with its picnic area and playing ground stands on five acres of ground reclaimed from the mudflats at the head of North Harbour in 1938. Above the Reserve at North Harbour Street a wooden footbridge built by the Balgowlah Progress Association in 1918 crosses over a shady gully to a pocket of thickly forested bushland at Wellings Reserve. In the 1880s two Aboriginal skeletons were discovered in the woods in stone lined graves. The Reserve is named after Leslie Wellings, a noted local historian and former Town Clerk of Manly.

The track continues past Forty Baskets Beach and Reef Beach to a lookout on Dobroyd Head, then past Grotto Point and the small sandy cove of Castle Rock Beach to Clontarf.

The City of Dublin in Ireland was known in ancient times as Clontarf, and was the scene of the battle in 1039 when the Irish expelled the Danes from Ireland.

St Patrick's dominates the Manly skyline like a feudal castle.

The sandstone walls of St Patrick's seem to glow in the late afternoon sunlight.

Stonemason's craftsmanship above the entry to the Seminary.

Clontarf

On the 12th March 1868 the 23 year old son of Queen Victoria, Prince Alfred the Duke of Edinburgh was the guest of honour at a formal picnic at Clontarf while visiting Australia during a world tour on board the warship *HMS Galatea*. The Duke was approached by Henry O'Farrell, an Irish supporter of the anti-royalist Fennian society, who produced a pistol and shot him in the back. The Prince staggered and fell crying 'Good God I am shot, my back is broken' as another of the guests, Mr Veal, grappled with and restrained O'Farrell. As luck would have it the force of the bullet was partly absorbed by the Prince's india-rubber braces, and he made a full recovery after being operated on a few days later at Government House. Veal was given a gold watch by the Prince when he recovered and in thanksgiving to the work of the doctors and nurses who saved his life, Alfred established a fund to build a hospital which was named the Royal Prince Alfred. O'Farrell had apparently acted on his own and his action was not supported by the Irish community in Australia. He was hanged in Darlinghurst Gaol on 21st of April that year.

From Clontarf the walk continues around Sandy Bay and Fisher Bay to The Spit bridge.

The Spit

The Spit is named after the sand spit that extends from the south shore of Middle Harbour. For 38 years from 1850 to 1888 Peter Ellery ran a hand punt service across the narrow channel of Middle Harbour from The Spit to the north shore. After Ellery retired a government steam punt provided a service on the crossing from 1889 until 1924 when the first toll bridge opened. In its last year of operation the punt carried 300,000 motor vehicles, 20,000 cycles and 50,000 horse drawn vehicles. The remains of a stone landing ramp used by the punt can be seen in the reserve on the north shore next to The Spit Bridge. The toll to cross the first Spit Bridge levied from its opening in 1924 until it was lifted in 1930 more than paid for the cost of the bridge and left a profit of over £5,000 used by Manly Council to widen the roadway on their side of the bridge.

The present Spit Bridge with its single lift span was opened in 1958. It lifts eight times a day during the week and thirteen times a day at weekends to allow passage for yachts and ferries through Middle Harbour.

Manly Reservoir

A tour of Manly wouldn't be complete without a visit to Manly Reservoir, accessible via King Street off Condamine Street (named after Thomas de la Condamine, Military Secretary to Governor Ralph Darling from 1828-31). Several walks meander through the surrounding bush. Swimming, boating and water-skiing are permitted on the lake and there are plenty of shady barbeque sites lining the west shore near the access road.

The lake dates to 1892 when work was completed of building a dam and pumping station across Curl Curl Creek to provide what was then expected to be a permanent freshwater supply for Manly village.

When Manly Dam ceased to be used as a water supply, the lake and surroundings were turned into a War Memorial Park in memory of those who had fallen in the First World War and other conflicts. An early map of the park shows the cove on the north shore of the lake pencilled in as Anzac Cove, and the fold of hills above, just below Allambie Heights, named Gallipoli.

North Harbour is on the coast track from Manly to The Spit.

Middle Harbour and The Spit Bridge. Clontarf is on right of picture.

Harbord to Long Reef

Stormy sunrise at Curl Curl.

Harbord to Long Reef

Scenes in the wilderness of Allenby Park behind Warringah Mall (above and right page).

Follow Condamine Street north from Balgowlah and at North Manly turn left on Kentwell Road then follow Allambie Road as it gently winds and climbs through Allambie Heights to the junction of Warringah Road. On the way you pass Gumbooya Reserve (Aboriginal for 'a peaceful place') where over two hundred Aboriginal carvings have been preserved. Shortly before the junction with Warringah Road, Aquatic Drive on the left leads to Warringah Aquatic Centre which has an Olympic class indoor swimming pool and diving pool and an outdoor pool. A good spot for a bathe if you prefer freshwater to saltwater.

Beacon Hill

Turning right on Warringah Road and driving down the long hill to Dee Why there's a view of the sea and beaches to greet your eye. When the road was planned in the 1930s, the Council recommended the present route of Warringah Road against one suggested by the Main Roads Board lower down the hill because 'the tourist public would miss the beautiful panoramic view obtainable from Beacon Hill'. Beacon Hill, 150 metres above sea level, was named after the erection in 1881 of a trigonometrical beacon called the Manly Trig station. Though we should think ourselves lucky that the hill is there at all. The shale on the west side of the hill was quarried away to provide the raw material for a nearby brick and tile works. Thousands of fossils of fish and plants were found during the time the quarry was in operation. Then in 1969 when the work was about to get underway of upgrading Warringah Road, the relevant authority planned to cut away the hill completely to make Warringah Road a straight line. Vocal local protests against the proposal were supported by Warringah Council, the road skirting the Hill was upgraded and widened instead and the Hill was preserved for posterity. A glance at the map shows the road gently curving round the Hill while the rest of Warringah Road between Narraweena and Frenchs Forest is a line as straight as a Roman road. From the car park at the base of Beacon Hill on Warringah Road a track leads to the top. Since 1931 the summit has been known as 'Governor Phillip Lookout'. Historians debate over whether Phillip actually ever climbed the Hill. The consensus of opinion is that he didn't, but the Hill overlooks the routes taken by Phillip and his companions during their explorations of the northern beaches.

The author J.H.M.Abbott once wrote of travelling to Manly and taking 'a tram to the pleasant Village of Brookvale – a straggling hamlet lying inland from the coast on the strip of littoral below the hills that rise into French's Forest' then walking up Beacon Hill Road and up the path to the top of Beacon Hill. Abbott mentioned an author, the late Grant Allen who wrote a book which he described as a 'hill-top novel', 'because its author thought it such a risque piece of authorship that only very daring people with no regard for conventions could afford to be seen reading it'. Abbott reckoned that if Grant Allen had ever climbed Beacon Hill, he would advise possible readers of his book to make an exception 'for if they went up there he would know they would not read any book that was ever written – unless they were blind, and it was a book in Braille'. Because 'There, on a flat platform of sandstone, you may spend an hour or more

Storm clouds seen from Governor Phillip Lookout.

in the enjoyment of one of the most beautiful outlooks that it is possible for you to come across in the neighbourhood of Sydney, or any other place'.

'Between yourself and the dark line of the northern water-shed of North Harbour is a great gulf of spacious atmosphere, paved with the valley of the Manly Lagoon, the golf links and vale of Balgowlah'. Beyond was a glimpse of Sydney Harbour, and 'In the south-east corner of the picture – a very much larger Village than it looks from The Corso – Manly straggles across its sandspit, and up the hills on either side. St Patrick's College, seems to dominate it like a feudal castle'. North of Manly:

> Freshwater, Harbord and Curl Curl are inhabited by a small portion of human beings, and immense hordes of weekenders… Curl Curl lagoon gleams behind its sandhills in the sunlight, as it winds into the flat valley bed, vividly green with Chinamen's gardens and nurseries, at the head of which lies Brookvale.
>
> Beyond the lagoon, a bulging headland, with nearly a mile length of cliff towering above the sea separates Curl Curl and Dee Why Beaches. Under the headland and of the hill, the little Dee Why village clusters amid the trees… Beyond Long Reef, the Pittwater Road winds around a long hog-backed, darkly wooded hill, beyond which lie Collaroy and Narrabeen Beaches.
>
> Past this high, dark hill, a blue-green haze of distance with a suggestion of purple in it colours the coastline… Headland after headland juts into the sparkling blue sea, until you pick out Barrenjoey, the South Head of Broken Bay…
>
> Inland to the North lies a wide relief map of low, rolling ranges, becoming an increasingly fainter blue that is only a little deeper in tone than the sky, as your eyes rest upon the limits of the world… dark ridges and blue valleys, beyond and beyond one another, until you see no more.

The view is still as magnificent as it was 60 years ago, and is unchanged except for a few more houses on the flats and the green of playing fields has replaced the green of Chinese gardens on the valley bed of Curl Curl Lagoon.

Brookvale

If we'd continued on Condamine Street instead of turning left on Kentwell Road, we'd reach the shopping centre of Brookvale. In 1899 there were just 40 householders in Brookvale, in 1911 the population was 200, and it wouldn't have been much higher in the 1920s when Vialoux passed through and described the settlement as 'a thriving little Arcadian village set in green gardens and comfortable homes, from which many beauty spots in the neighbourhood can be conveniently visited'. Vialoux also mentioned a

> little known beauty spot… Miles' Glen [accessed by] a bush track some 100 yards through a delightful jungle of verdant bush… By ascending the hill on the same track the Fall is soon reached…a lovely double cascade of water which drops down into a valley of mighty forest trees and sylven beauty equal to anything on the famous Blue Mountains…Wildflowers are in profusion all around, and the locality is a veritable sanctuary for our feathered singers.

Driving north towards the Northern Beaches it's easy just to dismiss Brookvale as seven sets of traffic lights on Pittwater Road, yet if we take Old Pittwater Road, and turn into Clearview Place then walk down the path at the end between two factories, we emerge into the 'little known beauty spot [of] Miles' Glen' exactly as Vialoux described it. The Glen and surrounding bush have been preserved as part of Allenby Park.

Early history

Brookvale was an unpopulated forested wilderness about five kilometres north of Manly when William Frederick Parker paid a deposit of £7 5s 0d to purchase

Rainforest in Stony Range Flora Reserve (above and top). The site was a rubbish dump infested with lantana when declared a reserve in 1957.

Sunrise at Freshwater Beach.

100 acres in the district on 11th January 1837. The following year Parker applied for the assistance of a convict on his estate and one Thomas Beedham was assigned to the task. By the 1880s the area had become known as Greendale, but the same name had already been given to a settlement south of Sydney (and since to one in Victoria) so to save confusion with postal districts, Greendale was changed to 'Brookvale' after the name Will Parker had given his house.

Stony Range Flora Reserve

Continuing through Brookvale and past the traffic lights at the junction of Warringah Road, a short distance on the right is the little sanctuary of Stony Range Flora Reserve, named after the stony range which is cut through by Pittwater Road at this point. Stony Range is one of those little treasures that can exist for years on your doorstep yet you remain oblivious to its existence. A bit like that old vase by the front door you keep the brollies in but which is in fact a piece of priceless Ming pottery. The reserve is a little pocket of rainforest with a countless variety of plants lovingly maintained by volunteers from the Manly Warringah Flora and Fauna Society.

Harbord

In 1818 Governor Macquarie made the first land grant in the district of 50 acres to Thomas Bruin. The Bruin estate, which became known as 'Freshwater', probably after the stream that runs between Wyuna and Wyndora Avenues, was bounded by present-day Evans Street, Albert Street and the approximate line of Undercliffe Road, and extended to high water mark on the beach.

The district remained virtually uninhabited except for one or two farms and the odd holiday shack until the first land sales in the 1880s. A land subdivision in 1886 was named Harbord in honour of the wife of the incumbent Governor, Lord Carrington. Her maiden name was Margaret Cecilia Harbord.

Camp City

From the early 1900s Freshwater was a popular destination as a working man's camp. On the flat ground inland from the beach men stayed first in tents, then in purpose-built weatherboard huts with galvanised iron roofs and basic furnishings of wooden tables, chairs and iron bunks. The huts went by names such as 'The Ritz' and 'Shark Bait'. Accommodation was for men only with lady visitors allowed only on Sundays. After the First World War new lodges or 'Camps' as they were still called opened catering mainly for working class families from Sydney. Many liked Freshwater so much they later returned to live, a particularly large community coming to stay from Balmain when the district was developed for housing.

'The Kiosk', the oldest building in Harbord built in 1908 on Undercliff Road overlooking the beach, dates to the era of the camps. It was built by Mr Lewers who owned and operated one of the camps and besides providing accommodation for visitors was a venue for afternoon tea parties, meetings and dances. When Harbord's first Post Office was established in 1909 it opened in the Kiosk. Lewers and Amos Randell, who operated some of the first camps on land he owned near Evans Street, with the assistance of the local Fishermen's Club, cut a path along the cliff at the south end of Freshwater Beach and blasted a tunnel through the rock of the headland. These days rock falls make access to the tunnel from the Freshwater side a bit of a scramble, but it can easily be reached by walking around the rocks past Queenscliff rock pool.

Freshwater Beach from the headland.

The Harbord Beach Hotel, built in 1928, is based on a South African design.

Previous page: Looking towards Manly from Freshwater Beach. Harbord Diggers Club is on the left.

To lift the status of the suburb above that of a campsite, Mr Jamieson the Shire Clerk of Warringah wrote to the Post Master General's Department on 17th August 1923 regarding having:

> the name of Freshwater changed to Harbord. Freshwater… has long fallen into disrepute on account of the people of doubtful and riotous character, who frequent the place at weekends in the summertime.

Another letter from the Council to the Officer in Charge of the police at Manly requested that bus operators changed their destination boards to Harbord and also 'be so good as to remove the name Camp City from the buses'.

So Harbord became the official name of the suburb and the beach again, though the beach was officially given back its title of Freshwater on 14th November 1980. The last of the camp lodges were sold in the 1930s and the sites sub-divided for housing. To ensure the appearance of the suburb lived up to its rejuvenated name, in the1930s Warringah Council designated the Harbord area between Brighton Street, Harbord Road and Queenscliff a 'brick area' and only brick homes have been built there ever since. Some of the more sturdy camp lodges were converted to cottages and they still exist today on some of the roads near the beach.

Freshwater Beach remained private property for nearly 100 years from the time of the original land grant in 1818 until it was resumed by the Government in 1910 for 'public recreation'. The rockpool at the north end, accessible by a short walk on a track below the cliff, was the first to be opened on the Northern Beaches in 1925.

Duke Kahanamoku

Freshwater's greatest claim to fame was in 1914, when Duke Kahanamoku asked a Sydney company to fashion a surfboard like the one he used in his native Hawaii, and gave the first demonstration of surfboard riding ever seen in Australia. In memory of this epic event there's a bronze statue of the Duke on a surfboard on the headland.

Duke Kahanamoku was even better known as a swimmer than a surfer and to name just a few of his endeavours, was the first man to swim 100 yards in under one minute and won medals at the 1912 Stockholm, 1920 Antwerp, 1924 Paris and 1932 (at the age of 42) Los Angeles Olympics.

The Duke's board on which he gave the first surfing demonstration at Freshwater was put on display in the Freshwater Surf Life Saving Clubhouse. When the Duke called at the Freshwater Club when he was in Australia for the 1956 Melbourne Olympics he took the board off the wall and showed everyone he hadn't lost his touch by riding the breakers once again.

The War years

During the war concrete tank traps were laid in a line west of the beach and barbed wire was strung in a maze formation across the sand. Swimmers could still use the beach, they just had to negotiate a way through the maze first! A searchlight crew was stationed on the dunes and as an exercise they would pick up the plane on the nightly flight from Sydney to Brisbane in the cross beams of their searchlights and hold it for as long as possible as it flew north.

Return to Albert Street and turn right. Soldiers Avenue on the left used to be Matheson Street but was renamed in 1922 following the First World War. Trees were planted in memory of fallen servicemen (some of which still exist). The first to be planted, on the corner of Soldiers Avenue and Oliver Street, was in memory of men from Freshwater Surf Life Saving Club who had paid the supreme sacrifice. On Wyuna Road four streets to the north a dairy farm with 60 head of cattle operated until the late 1940s. Harbord Park on Wyadra Avenue one street up is on land acquired by Warringah Council in 1927. The ground sloped towards the north, and during the depression men were employed on relief work to turn it into a level playing ground. A local, Jim Fleming recalled:

> Hundreds of men were employed shifting soil six feet in depth along the whole length of [the] Park... Little railroads were built from top to bottom, and the men filled small trucks and wheeled them down and back. Wages were 7/6 a week for single men and 18 shillings for married men... It was work of course, but so hopeless and pointless and I still remember the depressed expressions and attitudes of those men.

Next to the Duke's statue on the headland is the Harbord Diggers Club. The 'Diggers', opened on 7th March 1959, is something of an institution in the district. For a nominal membership fee members can enjoy the club's many sporting facilities, reasonably priced restaurants or have a spin on 'the pokies'. Buy why do people stand in front of a machine putting money in, when less comes out than what goes in? Interstate and overseas visitors can enter the club after signing the visitors' book. The Diggers is an ex-servicemen's club. Its forerunner was the Anzac Relief Division, formed by returned Diggers to help needy families during the Depression. Their activities included distributing surplus fruit and vegetables obtained from shops in Manly.

Harbord Surf Club. If it wasn't a surf club it would make a very desirable residence.

The biggest crowds at Freshwater and at every other beach in Sydney are on Boxing Day.

Flowers in a garden on Carrington Parade on the way to Curl Curl Beach.

Right page: Aerial view of Curl Curl Beach.

Curl Curl

Continuing around Lumsdaine Drive, join Carrington Parade and follow it to Curl Curl Beach. Francis Myers came this way in the 1870s, taking the coast route from Freshwater and

> swinging around by Curl Curl it opens up a great stretch of good and beautiful country, whose producing power is well shown by the garden at the head of the lagoon, which sends daily great crates of all garden produce to the village [Manly] and the city, everything useful and beautiful, from roses to cabbages.

In those days there was a patch of rainforest at the northern end of the beach which has since been engulfed by advancing sand dunes. The area around the lagoon which was such rich farmland in Myers' time and is now lush green parks and playing fields, wasn't so pretty in the 1960s. Six acres of swampland fringing the lagoon were the site of the old 'Curly Tip'. An earlier even greater threat to public health was the Curl Curl Rifle Range, set up by Manly Rifle Club in 1905 with targets mounted on the landward facing slope of the sand dunes. The Range was closed by the Defence Department in about 1920 because of the danger it posed to people using the beach.

Dee Why Head

Continue on Carrington Parade, crossing the bridge over Curl Curl Lagoon (Curl Curl incidentally, is Aboriginal for lagoon) into Griffin Road, then turn right at the traffic lights to take Huston Parade to the car park at North Curl Curl Beach. A track at the end of the carpark, neatly paved with crazy paving, leads to North Curl Curl Rock Baths. A branch off this track leads across the top of the cliffs for a half-hour walk to Dee Why.

Dee Why Lagoon

Continue on Griffin Road to Dee Why Beach. There's a great view of Dee Why and district as you crest the brow of the hill at Headland Road. Turn left on Dee Why Parade and right into the carpark behind the surf club. Dee Why Lagoon just beyond the carpark is a wildlife and bird refuge. There are still birds there today, but in nothing like the numbers there used to be, when the great flocks were like a cloud against the sun as they took flight.

The black swan is the symbol of Dee Why and a sandstone sculpture of the bird adorns the verge on Pittwater Road on both sides of Dee Why, but the creature is seldom seen today. In 1963 they took off en masse and left for regions unknown never to return. Was Beatles' music really that bad?

But the real reason is more prosaic. The wetlands surrounding the lagoon have mostly gone and large deltas have formed around the creeks entering the lagoon. Advancing urban development has meant rainwater run off is channelled to the sea by pipe instead of along the natural watercourses so there's no brisk run of water to flush sediment out of the lagoon. According to the Manly-Warringah Journal of Local History:

> This loss of depth and the consequential increased frequency of emptying of the Lagoon after rain because of its reduced storage capacity is probably the main reason that black swans are now a rarity. The seagrasses that they eat struggle to survive under these changed conditions.

Continue on the track round the lagoon and join Dee Why Beach at the point where the lagoon channel enters the sea. This is the junction of Dee Why Beach and Long Reef Beach, though it is in fact one long beach

Above: Dee Why Head and North Curl Curl. Curl Curl Lagoon joins Greendale Creek which meanders towards Brookvale.

Left page: South Curl Curl Rock Pool and Surf Club.

North Curl Curl Surf Club and Curl Curl Lagoon.

that's cut in two when the Lagoon channel is running after heavy rain. This stretch of beach is popular for windsurfers, and it's a great sight to see them skimming across the ocean at great speed or catching a wave and jumping high into the air when there's a stiff breeze blowing.

Dee Why

Return to the car via the beach, drive to the end of Dee Why Parade and turn left on Pittwater Road into Dee Why. The first land grant in the area was 500 acres issued to Mr William Cossar by Macquarie on 31st August 1819, comprising the land north of Dee Why Lagoon to Collaroy Beach and westwards towards Collaroy Plateau. The first known reference to Dee Why is a note written in pencil in Surveyor Meehan's field book 'Wednesday, 27th Sept,1815 Dy Beach – Marked a Honey Suckle Tree near the Beach'. A later survey by Meehan included the note 'Long Reef. Dy Lagoon, 12th April 1821'. Meehan was an Irish rebel transported for seven years to New South Wales for his part in the Dublin Uprising of 1798. Arriving in Sydney in 1800, and having had some training as a surveyor, he was immediately appointed an assistant to the Colonial Surveyor, a capacity he worked in energetically until his death in 1826. Meehan was very capable at his job, and was at times the 'Acting Government Surveyor' when the Government Surveyor was out of the colony. But why did Meehan pencil the letters Dy into his notebook? Was it to confound us because he never received the appointment of Government Surveyor he cherished? The question has certainly vexed historians ever since. Was it an abbreviation of the Greek dysprosium 'hard to reach' as no doubt Dee Why then was? Was it because the shape of the lagoon resembles the letters D and Y (I fail to see how) or that the letters were carved on a rock by a sailor from the Spanish ship *Dona Ysabel*

A spectacular sight on stormy days is the surf crashing onto the rocks in front of North Curl Curl Rock Pool.

Giant surf at North Curl Curl seen from Dee Why Head.

Surf breaking onto the rocks next to Carrington Parade.

Exciting free entertainment at South Curl Curl Rock Pool.

Dee Why Lagoon.

which once disappeared without trace in the Pacific (if they were, no one can quite remember where). I guess we'll never know.

The Jenkins Estate

But we do know that the history of Dee Why is closely tied in with that of the Jenkins family. When James Jenkins arrived in Sydney on the convict transport *Coromandel* with his brother William in 1802, they had less than two years left to serve of their seven-year sentences for allegedly stealing seven sheep. Following farming activities at Hunters Hill, a shipbuilding enterprise at Darling Harbour, and the murder of William by bushrangers, James started to buy up land holdings in the Collaroy area in the 1820s. In order to take his cattle and produce to market in Sydney, Jenkins built a road with 13 bridges (for years afterwards known as 'Jenkins Road') from Collaroy to the water's edge at North Harbour. Its route was roughly along Condamine Street, Old Pittwater Road and Pittwater Road. The square holes for the footings of some of Jenkins' original bridges can still be seen in the sandstone rocks of the creek beds they spanned.

When James Jenkins died in 1834, he left his estate to his wife and eight children. By 1892, only his daughter Elizabeth and youngest son John still survived, by which time the Jenkins' estate stretched in an unbroken line from Pacific Parade Dee Why to Mona Vale, amounting to a holding of approximately 1,840 acres. Elizabeth never married and seemed content to devote her life to religion and the Salvation Army cause. Following the crash of the banks in Sydney in the 1890s Elizabeth feared she may be exposed to debts she couldn't pay (in fact she wasn't liable) but asked the Salvation Army to accept liability in return for the transfer of most of the property owned by herself and John and an annual stipend for herself, John and several other family members. The land the Salvation Army received included 200 acres at Mona Vale, 500 acres at Collaroy and 200 acres at Dee Why.

The Salvation Army

The first task undertaken by the Salvation Army on its enormous estate was to build the 'Home of Rest' financed by a gift of £400 from Miss Jenkins. The building still stands today, it is the oldest in Dee Why, a charming structure with wide verandahs and a gabled roof, tucked behind the pine trees above Dee Why library. These days it is known as 'Pacific Lodge'. The Home of Rest was originally built as a recuperation centre for Salvation Army officers, its purpose, according to a Staff Captain of the day to throw

> its hospitable doors open to welcome weary warriors who have fallen in the fight [and provide an answer to] the harrassing question of the devil 'What will I do if I am taken sick'.

The Salvation Army expanded their activities in Dee Why, the 'War Cry' of 1912 detailing their enterprises. Coming into Dee Why from Manly on the right side of Pittwater Road was the Industrial Farm, which included separate buildings for a Boys' Home and a Home for Men temporarily in need of help. Across Pittwater Road was a Sanatorium for Men to care for 'inebriates'. Next along the road was a Home for Little Girls, and on the hill, the original 'Home of Rest' now used, with extensions, as a hostel for 50 aged men. Towards Collaroy was the Salvation Army's Hall, open to Salvation Army Officers and employees, the general public, and inmates of the homes. Flint Hayman recalled coming to the Industrial Farm as a boy in 1911 when his father was the Salvation Army Officer in charge and being told:

Dee Why Beach.

Aerial view of Dee Why Beach, with the golf links and low headland of Long Reef in the background.

Surf carnival at Dee Why.

Dee Why Beach and Surf Club. Beyond is the high ground of Beacon Hill, Narraweena and Cromer Heights.

Son, this place is impossible; eighty-odd in-bred jersey cows in a dairy… A large pig stye; about five acres of market garden; some 100 fowls at the North Narrabeen poultry farm. Most pathetic labour of old men, mostly alcoholics, and delinquent boys committed to the Institution by court order for some rehabilitation and training.

But concerns were being aired at this time by Warringah Council about the large landholdings in the district for the exclusive use of the Salvation Army, including Dee Why Beach, part of the original Jenkins' estate which the Salvation Army had fenced off as private property. In 1911, there were only five private dwellings in Dee Why. When a similar case had arisen at Harbord, where the beach was part of the holding of a previous land grant, the Government simply resumed the beach and that was that, but the Salvation Army were prepared to fight the Government in the courts to retain ownership of Dee Why Beach. However the Government won the case and the beach was opened to the public. Within two years the Salvation Army had closed their struggling Industrial Farm and started to sell off land for housing. Glasgow born 'General' James Hay, who arrived in Melbourne in September 1909 in command of Salvation Army activities in Australasia, was responsible for the Dee Why land and energetically set about surveying the area, arranging for it to be drained and sub-dividing it for the first land sales in the period 1911-14. This was the establishment of the town of Dee Why. Hay Street, parallel to Pittwater Road in Collaroy is named after the General, and Howard Avenue Dee Why honours a former Salvation Army Commissioner, Thomas Howard.

Dee Why sunrise.

Dee Why Beach

Once the beach was opened to the public in 1912 Dee Why Surf Life Saving Club was founded and a Surf Club opened. An early motion, passed during Dee Why Surf Club's annual meeting in 1913 stipulated that

no bathers be allowed to loiter on the beach unless, in the case of a lady, she is wearing : a kimono or like covering, and in the case of gents, a covering from neck to knee over their costumes.

Long Reef

From Dee Why continue north on Pittwater Road towards Long Reef. When Vialoux came this way he mentioned:

A walk from the tram stop at the Lagoon along the South Creek Road is a delightful experience… it is a painted road winding sweetly along under it canopies of green forest trees that lovingly overhang their branches as if to shelter and protect this path of Fairyland… (At) Wheeler's Estate… the path enters the primitive forest, with glorious giant trees lending dignity to the scene… It is to be hoped that these imposing giants will escape destruction when settlement comes along to this locality.

My daughter Juliette and our Dalmation 'Gwen' on the walk from North Curl Curl to Dee Why.

Alas, these days South Creek Road is an industrial estate, though Roche have preserved an area of flora in their factory grounds. And there are open spaces next to creeks, like at Dee Why Park and Cromer Golf Course, preserved because the original land grant of 1841 at Cromer stipulated 'all land within one hundred feet of high water mark on creeks, harbours or inlets' be reserved for 'public or naval purposes'. Cromer is named after 'Cromer Cottage' which stood approximately where the Golf Clubhouse now stands.

Enter Charles de Boos

At this point in the tale, it is timely to introduce one Charles de Boos, London born though claiming blue blood as the grandson of a French Huguenot count, who arrived in Sydney at the age of 20 and became a reporter with the *Sydney Morning Herald*. In 1861 he set off from Manly with two friends, Tom and Nat,

Who says it never snows in Sydney? The Dee Why Alps, St Kevin's Church on Oaks Avenue.

and a kangaroo dog 'Spanker' to journey to Palm Beach. As de Boos recalled:

> we were about to penetrate into an all but unknown country… the wild legends respecting it… have hitherto been regarded as fabulous… a district where stranger's visits are few and far between and where the foot of the tourist seldom treads. [But where he heard] 'Wallabi' scoured the bush in great flocks and would run over you if you did not get out of the way [and] wild ducks were so numerous that they were only too thankful to be shot.

The party walked through Manly beneath the gaze of Smith's stone kangaroo, which de Boos felt looked more like a 'coffee pot' than a kangaroo' then past the last farm and quitting 'the last vestige of civilisation… and forward into the wild, dark and unknown sea of leaves that moaned and rustled before [us]'.

As they trekked north, de Boos was surprised to find that even though so near Manly Beach, and with so much fine rich land around, the number of settlements should be so few.

> From the Manly Lagoon to the bridge over the head of the Deewy lagoon, I do not think we passed more than a half-dozen farms, and these were only very small holdings, producing nothing beyond corn and pumpkins, and looking just now more like poverty stricken and deserted tenancies…

Just beyond Dee Why de Boos crossed Jenkins' bridge over the creek next to the lagoon, which he found:

> Sufficient for the traffic that passes over it, although it must be somewhat dangerous to cross of a dark night in consequence as well as its narrowness as of the total absence of any handrail or side-guards.

Continuing east towards Long Reef, de Boos approached Jenkins' property, at that time occupied by Elizabeth Jenkins.

> This is the most beautifully situated homestead. The house, lying slightly back from the road is nestled in at the foot of a lofty and thickly timbered range, and has a beautiful lookout to the north, south and east, over the Pacific and over many of the bold headlands that breast its mighty rollers. This property includes a very large number of paddocks, all enclosed…

Long Reef Point

On our present-day journey, travelling north on Pittwater Road, after ascending the gentle hill next to Dee Why Lagoon and rounding the long sweeping corner to the left, the eye is greeted with a view of Long Reef golf links.

Turn right on Anzac Avenue and right again past Long Reef Golf Club House and Fishermans Beach to the 'Pay and Display' car parking area at the top. From the car park a track leads to the top of the headland. A notice on the way warns that this is Long Reef Aquatic Reserve, in which 'Marine wildlife is protected [and] taking, collecting, disturbing or destroying marine life, inter-tidal invertebrates or marine flora is prohibited' on Long Reef rock shelf and for 100 metres beyond low water mark. Ten minutes walk brings you to the summit where there's a drinking fountain and a strange assortment of rocks and ceramic designs paying homage to 'The Spirit of Long Reef Headland' where, 'On a quiet peaceful night you can hear the Long Reef Spirits singing in the ocean breeze'. At the top it's worth sitting down for a little while to make the most of the superb view towards Dee Why and Manly on one side and along the rocky headlands of the northern beaches on the other.

Driving up the road towards the car park you may have noticed that the low cliff of Long Reef headland has a distinct burgundy hue about it. Long Reef is quite different to the sandstone of the headlands of the rest of the Northern Beaches

Dee Why Rock Pool.

Big swells seen from the Rock Pool.

Fishermans Beach on Collaroy Basin. Long Reef is on the left.

The 'Colonial Heritage' on the rocks.

Ello ello what ave we ere. A speedboat on the rocks.

and according to geologists is a portion of the lip of a crater of a long extinct volcano. Many fossils have been found in the rocks, including the remains of a labyrinthodonts, a two metre long marine creature from the early Triassic period.

Two mines were burrowed beneath Long Reef at the end of the nineteenth century to search for copper ore, which was discovered, though not in commercially viable quantities. In places the waves have washed away the soft rocks of the headland to reveal outcrops of red ironstone, or as the author of the 'Geological excursion guide to the sea cliffs north of Sydney' puts it:

> Tertiary lateritic podzolic paleosal formed on both deltaic sediments of the lower Newport and Garie Formations, and underlying super-imposed grey-brown podzolic paleosols (ferrods) of the Bald Hill Claystone…

Long Reef golf links. Which are true golf links in the dictionary definition of the term as they are next to the sea.

Shipwrecks

The rocky headland of Long Reef has claimed many ships over the years. A glance at the map of the Northern Beaches shows Long Reef projecting beyond the line of other headlands like a leg sticking out ready to trip an unwary passer-by. There was the *Euroka*, wrecked in 1913 and abandoned, sections of which could still be seen on the reef in the 1950s. More recently, on 1st November 1997 the 18 metre *Colonial Heritage* ran aground and was holed, but successfully patched up and refloated. And in May 1998 a large speedboat belonging to a Sydney stock-broking identity motored onto the rocks, fortunately without mishap and the boat was refloated with no wounds except for a fractured propeller mechanism and a touch of injured pride. To placate the Spirit of Longreef some of Sydney's old ferries have been sunk in the waters off the reef, including the *Dee Why* scuttled in May 1966.

Setting off on the walk to Long Reef Headland.

Collaroy to Turimetta

Surfers entering the water at Collaroy Beach.

Collaroy to Turimetta

Sunrise at North Narrabeen.

Pelicans at Narrabeen Lakes.

Leaving Long Reef, follow Anzac Avenue to the end then turn right on Parkes Road and right again into Veterans Parade, named after the War Veteran's Home which you soon pass on the left. The Home has its own little war museum, accessible by Colooli Road. It is open 2.00 – 4.00 p.m. Wednesday, Saturday and Sunday and visitors are welcome. Veterans Parade traverses the top of Collaroy Plateau. In the 1880s Myers recommended that the visitor to Manly venture north on horseback and

> Gallop around the flat crown of Mount Ramsey [Collaroy Plateau] a plateau of 200 acres and on its seaward edge will ride carefully in places lest we crush the wild flower beds, which here seem set out as by most skilful gardeners' art, all colours delicately blended, and fringed by grey rock or dark green moss. We shall get down the precipice face easy enough, and descending, we shall find that it is not the rude, bold inaccessible bastion it appears, but a beautifully broken hillside, clothed with fig, and pittosporum, and oak, and innumerable ferns, with a dozen bowery gullies, down which trickle little streams, to waste themselves upon the broad green plain.

Jamieson Park

Edgecliffe Boulevarde off Veterans Parade skirts the edge of the precipice, and leads to the Edgar Gomall Wildflower Garden and McLean Lookout which both provide 180° views of Narrabeen. The road descends the precipice by Veterans Parade and Nioka Road. Turning left on The Esplanade at the bottom, then taking the track at the end into Jamieson Park leads after one or two minutes walk to a creek shaded by innumerable ferns just upstream from which is a bowery gully down which still trickles a little stream. Continuing on the path past the bridge over the creek, there's a picturesque walk leading along the shore of Narrabeen Lakes and through the woods to James Wheeler Place. You can return the same way, or make a round trip of it by returning to the car via Rose Avenue and Veterans Parade. If it's around lunchtime there are some barbecue spots near the lakeside in Jamieson Park. Another track starts from the carpark at the end of the Esplanade and heads east around the shore of Narrabeen Lakes, finishing after one or two kilometers at the bridge over the lakes on Pittwater Road. The track is a nice smooth one to take the kids for a bike ride because it's covered in bitumen, and to make a day of it there's a boatshed renting canoes, sailing boats and runabouts on the east shore of the lake.

Narrabeen

Returning to the car, continue on The Esplanade and Mactier Street then turn left onto Pittwater Road which soon leads to the shopping centre of Narrabeen.

> I dream tonight of Narrabeen beside the turquoise sea,
> The sweep of golden sunlit sand, white surf and windbent trees;
> The rippled lake so blue and still beneath the cloudless sky...
> In Narrabeen, in Narrabeen, There's joy in ev'ry breeze,
> There's laughter in the notes that come
> From out the sun-bathed trees...

Were the words Lilla McKay used to describe the district's charms in her song 'Narrabeen' published in the *Manly Daily* in 1924. But Phillip wasn't quite as enamoured with the charms of the lake when he led the first expedition this way on 15th May 1788, though he was enthused by his discovery of a black swan. As Phillip related to Lord Sydney in a despatch, we

> Found to the northward of this part of [Sydney] Harbour a large lake, which we examined, tho' not without great labour, for it is surrounded with a bog and large marsh, in which we were frequently up to the middle. There we saw a black swan; it was larger than the common swan, and when it rose, after being fired at, the wings appeared to be edged with white; there is some red on the bill, and it is a very noble bird. With great labour, in three days we got round the swamps and marshes...

A later traveller, was Lieutenant James Grant, who journeyed from Manly to Pittwater on 25th and 26th February 1801. Grant set off from Manly, sleeping the first night in a hut, then the following morning continued his march before daybreak

> ... till we came near to the banks of a stream, which the natives called Narrowbine... The stream, from the rain which had fallen during the night, and the tide of flood being in, as it was in the vicinity of the sea, was become deeper and more rapid than common... [Grant waded across with the water nearly up to his chin, though]. The bottom of the river was very rugged, with sharp-pointed rocks, which made us stumble and cut our feet; however we got over...

> [On the other side was an escaped convict, but] The poor creature gave himself up to me without condition... at this moment he presented a most pitiable sight, being literally almost starved, and had he got across the Narrowbine, he never would have been able to reach Sydney.

When George Caley the botanist passed this way in 1805 he called the lake 'Cabbage Tree Lagoon'. Then in 1815, when Surveyor Meehan mapped the south shore of the lake he called it 'Narrabang Lagoon'. Meehan stated that the name was Aboriginal for 'swan'. The high ground south of the lagoon (Collaroy Plateau) became known as 'Mount Ramsey' after the 410 acre land grant made to John Ramsey on 21st August 1818 by Governor Macquarie. Though Ramsey's financial difficulties led to the banks taking over his property in 1823. Then the property granted to James Jenkins at Narrabeen on 31st December 1831 was called 'Cabbage Tree Hill'.

However Narrabeen was the name that came into general use. As you drive through on Pittwater Road there's a sturdy wooden bus shelter on the left. This is the old tram shelter where D. H. Lawrence alighted on his journey to the Northern Beaches in 1922. Lawrence had caught the tram from Manly and thought

The boardwalk at North Narrabeen Rock Pool.

The track through Jamieson Park at Narrabeen Lakes.

A waterfall in Deep Creek Reserve on the north shore of Narrabeen Lakes.

The Wakehurst Parkway between Narrabeen Lakes and Oxford Falls.

Narrabeen was 'the end of everywhere, with new "stores" – that is, flyblown shops with corrugated iron roofs – and with a tram shelter and little house-agents' booths plastered with signs'. The tramline had been extended from Brookvale to the terminus at Narrabeen as a single line track in 1913. But the service lost money nearly every year of operation before finally closing in 1939.

Narrabeen Lakes

Continue through Narrabeen and cross the bridge over the lakes, then turn left onto the Wakehurst Parkway. There was no bridge at all over Narrabeen Lakes until the 1880s. The track crossed the lagoon by a ford marked with a row of piles on the east side of the crossing. Passengers were advised to rest their feet on the opposite seat as the horses hauled their carriage through the ford and water lapped beneath the doors. After heavy rain the lagoon was impassable and coach passengers were ferried across by rowboat and met by another coach on the opposite bank. A journalist with the *Sydney Morning Herald* was travelling through the Northern Beaches on 16th April 1880 for the ceremony to lay the foundation stone of Barrenjoey Lighthouse. The three carriages carrying the dignitaries and guests reached Narrabeen, and according to the story in the following day's paper:

> The passage of the lagoon was, however, rather exciting to most of the party, from the fact that hints had been thrown out beforehand that the horses might jib and leave us in the middle of the water… Frequent inquiries were made of the ladies as to whether 'their feet were wet yet', as the bottom of the body of their vehicle seemed to be immersed…

The Wakehurst Parkway

If your tour for the day is finished the Wakehurst Parkway makes an alternative route to return to Manly or Sydney. It's one of the most picturesque stretches of road on the Northern Beaches, so it's worth describing some of the features on the way.

The road first skirts Narrabeen Lakes next to Bilarong Reserve. When Myers came through in the 1880s he found Narrabeen was still a wilderness of bush, trees and wildflowers, 'figs growing banyan like, forming… avenues, arches and bowers, so dense they might well be termed grottoes, deep cool grottoes of leafy boughs'. And as there was no one

> to hack and hew and desecrate the bush, it is all a delightful wilderness. Take advantage of it now as it is, for surely as human nature will seek to surround itself with natural beauty, it will become an outpost of the great city ere long.

Thankfully, much of the nearby land is still native bush, and local land zoning has been put in place to preserve most of the Lagoon surroundings.

Deep Creek Reserve

After one or two kilometres, travelling by car on the Wakehurst Parkway, a turnoff on the right leads to Deep Creek Reserve. There's a park reserved for dog training, and a waterfall cascades over the cliff at the head of the Reserve. A track on the left crosses Deep Creek by a bridge then follows a pipeline to a junction where you turn right. Stay on the track then turn left where it meets Deep Creek once more, and follow it through some dense bush for about 20 minutes to some little cascades. The easiest way from here is just to turn back the same way, but you can bush-bash to the left (south) to a horse trail on the ridge that'll take you back down to the Wakehurst Parkway. An interesting and adventurous alternative was recommended in a 1930s book on walks in the Northern Beaches called 'Hiking for Health'. The 25 kilometre trek was called by the author 'no walk for novice or new-chum bush-walkers… This is the roughest, the most beautiful walk in the whole of the Warringah area'. Described here in the opposite direction outlined in the book, the walk involved bush-bashing along the length of the course of Deep Creek all the way to Forest Way near the junction of Mona Vale Road, then completing a circuit by walking down Tumble Down Dick Hill to Mona Vale and returning to your starting point via Pittwater Road and the road by Narrabeen Lakes.

However, continuing our journey by car along the Wakehurst Parkway, after crossing the bridge over Deep Creek, near a track that leads into the bush on the right are the remains of some round concrete structures. In 1888 Mr W. Williams sunk two bores here to prospect for oil. No oil was found, but each bore one at a depth of 1,000 feet and the other at a depth of over 2,000 feet, hit natural gas. A gasometer was built and supplied for a time some of the local properties before the operation closed down. Curiously, the volume of gas produced at high tide was greater than at low.

Cascades on Oxford Creek.

Oxford Falls

The Wakehurst Parkway continues along the lakeside, past the New South Wales Academy of Sport on the left, then through three or four kilometres of virgin bush to Oxford Falls. This section of road is impassable after prolonged periods of heavy rain, and under these conditions a floodgate is swung across to close the Parkway at Oxford Falls and near the Academy of Sport. We can't have the ladies getting their feet wet. Turn off to the right on Oxford Falls Road West, and the falls are next to the road where it crosses Middle Creek by a ford. There's a footbridge for pedestrians. A more picturesque series of three waterfalls in a bush setting next to some barbecue sites can be found by continuing to the end of Oxford Falls Road West past the giant satellite dishes and turning right into the Recreation Reserve on Oxford Creek.

The lower cascades on Oxford Creek.

In the early days Oxford Falls was known as Bloodwood Gully after the giant eucalypts in the district which dripped red sap like the blood from a wound. Then in 1902 the settlement was renamed Oxford Falls after a 200 acre grant belonging to Alexander Bowman known as 'Oxford Township'. One of the first descriptions of the area was given by George Caley, the botanist, who arrived in Sydney in April 1800 at the behest of the director of the Royal Gardens at Kew in London, Sir Joseph Banks, to collect seed and plant specimens. Caley set off on an overland journey from West Pennant Hills on 18th February 1805, marching through the woods and bush to the sea, and arrived at Narrabeen Lagoon. On his return journey he crossed the cascades at Oxford Falls and described them in his field book. Three types of Grevillea collected by Caley on this journey are now in the herbarium of the Natural History Museum in London. They can still be seen growing in their natural environment along Mona Vale Road and at Collaroy Plateau.

Inaccessible Oxford Falls, surrounded by the rock ridges of Warringah Plateau, was only settled in any numbers in the early part of this century. The Wakehurst Parkway didn't then exist and the only access was by a rough track, frequently impassable in wet weather, leading down from Warringah Road. By 1928 the population was 64 people in nineteen households. They were true pioneers, eking out an existence growing vegetables in smallholdings or by poultry farming. The settlement had its own school, and church, built in a day with a working party under the direction of Anglican preacher Percy Gledhill (he was also an author, mentioned elsewhere in this publication). That same year a local resident John MacGregor offered some of his land as a site for a tennis court and the bush was cleared but a dispute erupted over sport on Sundays and the project foundered. It wasn't until 1935 that Oxford Falls was connected by electricity, whereas Newport, much further north, was connected in 1930.

Even today the district seems to exude a kind of pioneer spirit. Development of much of the surrounding bushland has been frozen and zoning laws have preserved the low density development pattern of the area. A drive along Oxford Falls Road presents us with the pleasant sight of horses grazing in fields, stables, a little rustic church and houses on large properties. Oxford Falls was only connected to reticulated water in the 1980s. The school closed in 1986 when there were no longer enough pupils for it to be viable. Newer residents often have a dollar to spend and are looking for a rural retreat within commuting range of the city.

Frenchs Forest

Continue on the Wakehurst Parkway to the junction of Warringah Road in Frenchs Forest. These days it's a busy intersection with traffic lights but for years the junction was known as the 'Blinking Light' after the blinking light that was strung across the dangerous cross-roads at a time when there were no street lights. In the 1960s the Beacon Hill Progress Association suggested the name 'Blinking Light' should be officially adopted for the junction, but the council didn't favour the proposal because 'blinking' in those days was considered an impolite form of expression.

In the 1880s Francis Myers recommended to the visitor to Manly

Collaroy Rock Pool. In the background are the Surf Club and the Collaroy Twin cinema, with the slope of Collaroy Plateau rising behind.

Auntie Jill and Juliette enjoying the view of Bantry Bay from Frenchs Forest.

Pittwater Road at Collaroy.

Fishermen on the storm water outfall at Collaroy Beach.

Right Page: Beachfront properties line Collaroy and Narrabeen Beach.

[If] you weary of fishing by two or three in the afternoon, take a horse or trap and make a way along the branch from the main Sydney Road towards Frenchs Forest. It is a wild country, when once the main road is left, stones and scrub, and stunted useless timber. Truly it might be said a wasteland, where no man comes or hath come, since the making of the world.

There weren't many trees when Myers passed because they'd already been cut down by James Harris French after whom the district is named. French, a Special Constable and Ranger of Crown Lands originally from Dorset, bought land in the area and developed a sawmill industry. Giant trees were cut and split by manual labour then hauled by bullock cart to his sawmills in the present vicinity of Warringah Road. The sawn timber was then shipped to Sydney or elsewhere on the Harbour from a wharf on Bantry Bay. In 1867 French married a daughter of Billy Blue, the famous Negro convict who rowed the first 'ferry' across Sydney Harbour from Millers Point to Blues Point.

Settlement in Frenchs Forest only really got under way during the First World War, when the government granted 70 blocks of land as part of a Soldiers' Settlement Plan. Conditions were tough, with no electricity or running water, and the soldiers had only their pensions to fall back on, but there was a will there and the settlement became permanent. These noble pioneers even founded a short-lived newspaper in 1917, the '*French's Forest Fonograph*'. By 1920, Frenchs Forest had a population of 115 souls. Vialoux noted in 1922:

the happy progress [of the] Soldiers' Settlement, which affords much gratification to the visitor who has the welfare of our brave Diggers at heart. Many fine orchards are to be found in the Forest, and settlement is extending rapidly in this rich and beautiful territory.'

Some of the Diggers' original humble dwellings with wide verandahs and gable roofs are still standing in the suburb of 'Forestville'.

Bantry Bay

From the end of Grattan Crescent in Frenchs Forest a bush track descends down the bluff to Bantry Bay then climbs through the bush at Seaforth and runs parallel to the Wakehurst Parkway to return to its starting point via Bantry Bay Road. On Bantry Bay the track passes the remains of the wharf from which French used to ship his timber, and as it climbs to Seaforth the track follows the old road to the wharf. Close to the Wakehurst Parkway near Seaforth Oval an imposing monument with a robust bronze plaque celebrates the opening of the Parkway by Lord Wakehurst on 22nd March 1946. Work started on the road as a relief work for 300 unemployed men during the Depression in September 1934. There was only one compressor to operate the pneumatic drills for drilling and blasting operations so a double shift was worked. In March 1942 when a Japanese invasion seemed a real threat, work on the road closed down and the men were moved to Mona Vale to make tank traps and erect shore defences. Work

Narrabeen Head and Narrabeen Lakes.

started again in March 1945 and a belated opening amidst great fanfare took place at the monument a year later.

Just behind the monument the 'Engravings Track' follows the route of French's old timbergetters trail. There are many deep scratches on exposed rocks left over from the days when the bullock trains dragged the heavy logs over this route to the sawmill. On the left, shortly before the track joins Bantry Bay Road, are a collection of Aboriginal rock engravings. There are eighty or more impressions, including a dingo, an echidna, snakes, whales, fish, boomerangs, axes and clubs, a bark canoe and a shield. But sadly, many of these carvings have now been all but obliterated by the elements.

Continuing on our journey by car on the Wakehurst Parkway, the road passes the bush of Manly Dam Reserve and soon reaches the shopping centre of Seaforth from where it's an easy run down Sydney Road to Manly or down Manly Road to Sydney via The Spit. Which sounds like a contradiction in terms!

The track on the south shore of Narrabeen Lakes.

Collaroy

An alternative and just as scenic route to Narrabeen from Long Reef is via the beaches. Turn right from Anzac Avenue onto Pittwater Road and coast down the gentle hill into Collaroy shops. On the way you pass on the left the Salvation Army Conference Centre and Home for the Aged, built on land that was part of the original Jenkins' gift to the Salvation Army. Junius took this way in 1861, heading to Pittwater on horseback, which he found was the only way to get there other than on foot. Writing in the *Sydney Morning Herald* on 6th April 1861 he told how:

Passing Jenkins' farm there is a level piece of beautiful turf nearly two miles long

Looking across to the ocean from Narrabeen Lakes. The small park on the point in the foreground is known as 'Wimbledon Reserve'.

69

Narrabeen town centre. Pittwater Road crosses Narrabeen Lakes at the bridge.

Looking towards Collaroy from North Narrabeen. Narrabeen Lakes enters the sea at the channel on the right.

and a quarter of a mile broad, quite fitted for a racecourse; forming, the finest gallop anywhere near Sydney.

Pittwater Road follows the line of the level turf through Collaroy and Narrabeen.

Ruth Park in her novel 'The Harp in the South', published in 1948, describes the journey of Roie and Charlie, who are travelling to Narrabeen for their honeymoon. '... the bus spun downwards into Collaroy, past a theatre like an exotic lime ice cream. And soon it was impatiently chugging, waiting for them to get off at Narrabeen Village'. At least in 1948 the buses stopped in Collaroy, in 1906 when the first Motor Omnibus service commenced operations, there were so few houses and so few people ever got off there that the bus company received complaints that this new fangled mode of transport 'frequently didn't stop at all at places like Collaroy'.

The old Collaroy Picture Theatre built in 1938 still stands on Pittwatre Road and is still showing movies, though these days it goes by the name of the 'Collaroy Twin' and is painted a frightful shade of cyan. The theatre is just across the road from the beach and the stage is below sea level. For three weeks during construction water pumps were used continuously until the concrete footings were brought up to street level.

Almost all the settlements on the Northern Beaches are set back from the beach with a reserve between the breakers and the first houses. Somehow at Collaroy, through the ministrations of a developer or because of a lack of civic foresight, the east-west streets end at the sand of the beach and the houses on Pittwater Road and Ocean Street are built right on the beach front. And at a

Looking north towards Turimetta and Mona Vale from North Narrabeen. North Narrabeen Surf Club is on the lower left of picture.

Looking towards Mona Vale from Turimetta Head.
Previous page: Early morning light at Turimetta.

Grey heron at Turimetta Head.

Sulphur crested cockatoo on the cliffs at Turimetta.

price. On 11th June 1945 an enormous storm swept the beach and houses at the south end were threatened by the waves. Walls of sandbags were built and even tank traps placed to repel an expected Japanese invasion were hurled onto the sand to try to hold back the sea. But once Mother Nature makes up her mind about something there's no stopping her, and it was all to no avail. Eight houses were destroyed, one of them actually floated out to sea, while another, later re-erected across the street, was actually moved halfway to its new destination by the force of the waves. The council declared that section of the shore just south of Fraser Street a danger area not to be built on and it has remained a reserve ever since. Storms threatened the beach again in 1967, when truckloads of rubble were tipped onto the sand to save the foundations of the tall white block of flats on Ramsey Street.

A ship wreck

The crescent of sand stretching north from Collaroy is, at nearly four kilometres, the longest of the Northern Beaches, but it is in fact two beaches, in name at least, Collaroy at the south end and Narrabeen at the north. The beach was always known as Narrabeen and Collaroy didn't exist until a coastal paddle steamer of that name lodged in the sand. On 20th January 1882 the *Collaroy*, named after an Aboriginal word for 'long swamp reeds', was sailing south off the coast during a storm. The wind and waves drove the ship close in to the shore at Long Reef, and the Captain, seeing he wasn't going to make it round the rocks, ran the ship aground onto the beach. The crew struggled ashore with no loss of life, though one of the sailors suffered a broken leg. No one lived near the beach in those days so they set off in the direction of Manly and knocked on the door of the first house they came to, the Jenkins' homestead.

Elizabeth Jenkins answered the door and one of the crew requested the loan of her horse and cart to take the injured man to hospital, but she refused on the grounds that if he'd been at home reading the Bible as he should have been he wouldn't have broken his leg in the first place.

The ship remained stuck fast in the sand for over two and a half years, defying all attempts to pull her free, until 19th September 1884 when a new owner who had a soap and candle factory in Sydney, liberally greased her hull with soap and wax and finally wrenched her from the sand. One man was killed by a whipping cable in the operation. The *Collaroy* was transformed into a sailing ship by the removal of her paddles and engines and the addition of an extra mast and pressed into service for the trade between North America and Australia. But the ship seemed to be cursed. In June 1889 she ran into difficulty again near the Humbolt Reef off the west coast of America. There was no soft beach in sight to run onto this time and she was dashed onto the rocks. One of her anchors was retrieved and now graces the schoolyard at Narrabeen. The name Collaroy stuck as fast to the south end of the beach as the ship had stuck in the sand.

North Narrabeen Beach

Continuing in the car north on Pittwater Road, branch off to the right on Ocean Street. Ocean Street runs parallel to the beach, and any of the 12 side roads you pass on the right leads to the beach and the sparkling blue Pacific. Ocean Street crosses the lagoon entrance by a bridge, then the thirteenth turn-off on the right leads to North Narrabeen rock baths and Narrabeen Head. At low tide you can paddle across the water of the lagoon to North Narrabeen Beach. Near the bridge on Ocean Street canoes are available for hire on holidays and at weekends. The

A typical tranquil summer afternoon at Turimetta Beach.

'Pelican Path' leads along the north shore of Narrabeen Lakes from Ocean Street, and winds round via Pittwater Road to Narrabeen. A stroll along Waterloo Street and North Narrabeen Beach takes you back to your starting point.

Narrabeen Head

From the car park at North Narrabeen a sturdy flight of wooden steps leads to the top of Narrabeen Head, a good vantage point for the view along the length of Narrabeen Beach. On 5th December 1909 George Augustine Taylor made his first flight in a heaver-than-air machine from Narrabeen Head. Francis Myers in 'A Traveller's Tale from Manly to the Hawkesbury' (1858) mentions 'It is possible to ride from Manly to Narrabeen at low tide along the beaches and picnic at the north end of Narrabeen Beach'. Though the road was rough 'the beauty of the place makes the aches and pains [of the journey] pale into oblivion'. In the 1940s there was a stables and riding school at the corner of Ocean and Octavia Streets Narrabeen. Riders used to gallop their charges along the length of Narrabeen Beach.

Turimetta Beach

The track crosses the Recreation Reserve on the Headland to a lookout with a view of Turimetta Beach. Turimetta is one of the smallest and least known but most picturesque of the Northern Beaches. It is tucked away out of view of the main road, and you'll only catch a glimpse of the beach if you turn right onto Narrabeen Park Parade. There is no suburb of Turimetta, or a street name except for a little side turn in Mona Vale, so if you talk about Turimetta there are even many Northern Beaches residents who will look at you blankly. Some steps off the track lead down to Turimetta Beach, and at low tide you can walk over the rocks below Narrabeen Head to North Narrabeen to return to the car.

Turimetta Head

Continuing on the track above Turimetta Beach leads through the heath land of Turimetta Head to a lookout. It's well worth the extra effort because the lookout on Turimetta Head is even more spectacular than that on Narrabeen Head. Not only are there views south all the way to Manly but also north to Mona Vale and the headlands towards Palm Beach. North Narrabeen and Turimetta Head used to be known as Sheep Station Hill. The grassy slope was used for sheep grazing when the land was part of the original Jenkins' estate. When the property passed to the Salvation Army and it was sub-divided for housing some of the streets were named after Salvation Army officers, including Arnott Crescent and Carpenter Crescent. Arthur Arnott was a son of the Arnotts, founders of the biscuit bakers, and became a Salvation Army Captain. The firm honoured their Salvationist member by calling two of their products after him. Thin Captain and SAO biscuits, the latter standing for the Salvation Army motto 'Serve and Obey'.

An aerial view along the Northern Beaches from Turimetta. The headlands look like a line of locomotives waiting to leave a railway siding.

Warriewood to Bungan

Paragliders on the Recreation Reserve above Mona Vale Beach.

Warriewood to Bungan

Angry surf on the rocks south of Warriewood Beach.

From Turimetta Head the track leads down the hill to Warriewood Beach. Land fronting the beach was originally promised to Alexander McDonald by Macquarie in three separate grants in 1813, 1816 and 1821 totalling an area of 81 hectares. Not long after receiving the last grant, on 21st December 1821 McDonald was drowned with his wife and son-in-law when their boat overturned on the Parramatta River, apparently during a drunken quarrel.

The area behind Warriewood and Mona Vale on the west side of Pittwater Road was once known as 'Crystal Valley' after the thousands of glasshouses that supplied the Sydney markets with fresh vegetables and cut flowers. The glasshouses and neighbouring market gardens were established by European migrants arriving after the First World War, many of them from Italy and Yugoslavia. Farming remained profitable especially for tomatoes, until the 1960s, when mass production in Queensland and advances in overnight transport led to the decline of the industry. Some market gardens and now mostly derelict glasshouses still exist, and can be seen on a drive through Garden Street and MacPherson Street Warriewood to Mona Vale Road.

Powder Works Road

Powder Works Road off Garden Street is a picturesque short cut to Mona Vale Road. The road winds and gently climbs through the leafy suburbs of North Narrabeen and Elanora Heights to Ingleside, with glimpses through the trees on the right to Mona Vale.

For the name that graces the road, we are indebted to Carl Von Bieren. He arrived in Sydney with his rich American wife in 1882, claiming to be a graduate of the University of Heidelberg and a student of the School of Mines in Freiburg. On the heights above Narrabeen on Manor Road Von Bieren built 'Ingleside House' a Tyrolean timber chalet with thirteen rooms which had a fine view to the ocean. With finance raised through a share offering, Von Bieren established the Australian Powder and Explosives Manufacturing Company in the deep gully close to his home. When Myers passed through he described the powder mills as

> the first in the colony (but)... also the most extensive and complete in the southern hemisphere... Everything that capital could command and ingenuity devise has been obtained and adopted... down in substantial stone building, separated from each other by breadths of turf... men dressed in flannel garments pursue their black art...

To celebrate the first setting off of a gunpowder charge from the factory, Von Bieren prepared to toast the occasion at a function at his chalet attended by the Governor Lord Loftus and the Premier Sir Henry Parkes. The guests gathered on the verandah to view the setting off of the explosive charge, the fuse was lit, but at the crucial moment, after a welter of anticipation, there was nothing but a deathly silence. A labourer was despatched to investigate, but when he reached the charge it exploded blowing up the poor man with it.

In 1885 just as commercial production of gunpowder was about to commence Von Bieren ran out of money. He travelled to Melbourne claiming he was going to raise further capital, but instead boarded a ship for Margate, England under

Warriewood Beach. At low tide you can walk over the rocks below the headland to Mona Vale Beach.

Turimetta Head from Narrabeen Park Parade. Warriewood Surf Club is on the right.

Above: Early morning surf at Warriewood.

Left page: Looking west from Warriewood. The white dome of the Bahai temple can be seen on the horizon.

The view of Warriewood Beach from Turimetta Head.

the name of 'Mr Walbridge'. Sergeant Murphy of the local constabulary was hot on his tail, and boarded a faster ship for the same destination, so that when Von Bieren alighted in Margate there was Murphy waiting to arrest him. Von Bieren was escorted back to Australia to stand trial, and found guilty of fraudulently embezzling a bankdraft of £799. Sentenced to 18 months hard labour, in consideration of his plea that he was incapable of it due to indigestion the judge added another ten months to his sentence.

It turned out Von Bieren was actually the illegitimate son of a Mr Walbridge, a servant of the real Von Bieren. He is rumoured to have spent his last days in San Francisco.

Ingleside House became derelict and then caught fire, however a stone gatepost decorated with a carved gun barrel and the words 'Advance Australia' still stands next to the road. Perhaps old 'Carl' would sit up in his grave if he knew they were the words later used in the title of Australia's National Anthem.

Mona Vale

Above Warriewood Beach follow Narrabeen Park Parade to the Recreation Reserve on top of the headland separating Warriewood and Mona Vale Beach. There's a view of Mona Vale Beach and Golf Course, and in the distance Pittwater sparkles between the fold of hills on each side. Colourful paragliders sometimes take off from the Reserve and glide over the beach on the sea breeze. Continue on Coronation Street past Mona Vale Hospital and turn right on Pittwater Road.

The Bahai Temple

Pittwater Road continues past picturesque Mona Vale Golf Course and the bowling club to Mona Vale Road. The road heads out through the houses of Mona Vale, then is soon meandering and climbing through the bush to the Bahai Temple at

A waterfall on Mullet Creek is accessed by a path leading off Irrawong Road North Narrabeen.

Following the creek up from the waterfall leads to this rainforested gully.

Bush scenery along Mullet Creek.

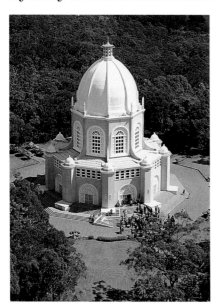

The congregation leaving the Bahai Temple after Sunday service.

the top of Tumble Down Dick Hill. The white painted domed temple, shining in the sun like a white beacon above the surrounding bush, was built by the Bahaists in 1961. They are a peaceable sect welcoming all-comers who preach the oneness of mankind and equality for all. Bahai temples have been built in the seven continents, and that at Mona Vale represents the faith in Australia and Oceania.

As you rush up 212 metre high Tumble Down Dick Hill with no more effort than a slight depression of the right foot on the accelerator, spare a thought for the poor horses which used to haul their loads up the steep climb under a blazing sun. At the top of the hill hewn out of the rock there's still a water trough where they used to quench their thirst.

Duffy's Forest

When nearby Duffy's Forest was first offered for sale at public auction in 1856, there were no takers and the following year the Government granted 100 acres to Mr P. J. Duffy for timber cutting. Timber was shipped to Sydney via a stone wharf on Cowan Creek, and to the coast down Mona Vale Road. The story goes that the bullock teams dragging the timber down the hill were led by a blind horse affectionately known as Dick. One day Dick lost his footing and tumbled down the hillside, breaking his neck, and the hill has been known as Tumble Down Dick ever since. Locals claim his skeleton remained where he fell for many years as a kind of macabre monument.

The Rock Lily

Coming into Mona Vale on Pittwater Road, look out for a little single storey brick structure with bay windows on the left hand side of the road. This is the Rock Lily Inn, built in 1886 by a bearded 20 stone timber getter from Warriewood, Leon Houreaux. Houreaux bought four acres of land at Mona Vale and built an inn to cater for the burgeoning tourist trade of daytrippers who travelled up by coach from Manly at weekends. He christened his coaching inn the 'Rocklily' after the rock orchids or 'rock lilies' which grew in the local bush. Under the guiding hand of his manageress, Madame Boutin, the hotel did a flourishing trade. Houreaux's dishes were the stuff of legends, and seemed to be of a flavour quite unknown to the clientele. Some of the ingredients were said to be snakes, possums and other 'game' from the nearby forest. In case visitors tired of the food, adorning the walls were brightly painted colour murals brushed by Houreaux himself, including gory battle scenes from the Napoleonic wars and in a backroom, out of sight of the ladies, there were even more colourful pictures. The Inn gained such a reputation for rowdy behaviour that the neighbours finally tired of all the noise and carryings on and had the Inn licence revoked by Local Option Poll in 1913. The Inn has gone through various incarnations since including a dance hall but has recently been restored and re-opened as a restaurant.

Charles de Boos at Mona Vale

The suburb of Mona Vale takes its name from 'Mona Vale Farm' which was built in the 1820s close to the beach. On their third night out from Manly, de Boos and his entourage were invited to stay with the Lush family at the Mona Vale Farm on the northern side of present-day Darley Street. The lady of the house shared the evening meal with her guests and the following morning her son Frank offered to take de Boos and his friends on a 'Wallabie' and duck shoot. Returning to the house that night empty handed, Frank already having headed home, de Boos recalled:

Mona Vale from Bongin Bongin Bay.

Mona Vale Rock Pool is on the rockshelf between Bongin Bongin Bay and Mona Vale Beach.

A pelican has just left it's bundle by the Rock Pool. I wonder if the lady was expecting it.

Surf boats riding the waves at Mona Vale Beach.

We were about to enter the garden gate, when we suddenly heard a bow – wow – wow! a short distance to our left. "The dog has tree'd a possum." Said Tom… so we hurried over to where one of the dogs of our host stood barking excitedly under a tree, making occasional desperate attempts to climb up. I looked up, but could see nothing. Tom, however, examined the tree carefully, and then suddenly exclaimed, "By Jupiter, I see his eyes!" I looked to where he pointed, and certainly there could be no mistake about the eyes, for there they were, like two red coals of fire. In an instant, Tom's gun was at his shoulder, a flame and a report, and then followed a wild demoniac shriek, such as certainly never came from the throat of an opossum,… We were not left long in doubt. Catching wildly at the branches amongst which it crashed in its descent, it came to the ground with a heavy thud and the dog at once sprang at it. He sprang at it quickly, but more quickly did he spring back again, uttering loud yelps of pain. We ran up, and seeing the wounded animal struggling on the ground, I dropped the butt of my piece upon it, and so rubbed it out. Tom then caught it by the tail, and held it up to examine it, when, by the little light given out by the stars we were just able to perceive that we had shot our host's cat. With feelings very nearly akin, as I should imagine, to those experienced by murderers, we held a hurried consultation, in which we mutually recognised the necessity for secrecy, and in pursuance of which we performed the funeral obsequies of poor Pussy at once and on the spot.

We rooted a whole in a sandhill with the butts of our fowling pieces, deposited the body therein, and hastily covered it over with the sand, which we trod down with our feet. This done, we returned towards the house, with somewhat relieved, but far from easy minds… Of course on entering we were questioned as to what we had fired at, and our 'possum shooting on such a night became the theme upon which no small quantity of jokes was based…

[later] Tom was in the midst of the most interesting portion of his colloquy with the old lady, by which he was eliciting thunders of applause from the juvenile portion of the audience, when suddenly there came a mysterious thwack against the door, followed by the growl of a dog… Tom turned deadly pale, as he dismissed the ancient lady most ignominiously; "What the deuce is the matter?" said our host, as he sprung to the door, where the shaking and bumping seemed to be going on vigorously. His question was answered as soon as the door was opened, and the light streamed upon the scene that was enacting. There was the deceiver of a dog that had led us into our difficulty – [with the] cat which had been the pride of the household and the especial favorite of its mistress. In our haste, we had thought only of the cat, and had forgotten all about the dog, of whom we had altogether lost sight after his yelping retreat. He, however, had not lost sight of us, and being determined to have some kind of satisfaction for the clawing he had received about the nose, had scratched up pussy's carcase, to which our slovenly burial offered no very great impediment, and had brought it up to the house, so that he might have the agreeable amusement of shaking it every now and again whenever the pain of his nose reminded him of the insult he had undergone. The children at once rushed forward and claimed the carcase, now caressing the once lively favorite, and now addressing Tom with "Oh, Mr Tom, how could you!"… our hostess said nothing, but she looked daggers… "Well," said Frank, "you are a nice sportsman!" "Yes," responded Tom, looking down demurely at the cat; "it was a pity, wasn't it?" Here, of course, we had a world of lamentations over the poor animal, all its amiability, all its virtues and good qualities were set forth, each vying with the other in their anecdotes…

[returning to their quarters and] summing up the events of the day, we could hardly come to the conclusion that it was calculated to add to our sporting honours. We had missed the ducks and had shot a cat. I [soon] was sound asleep. It needed not the lullaby sung by the waves, as with low moans they broke upon the beach, to send me off to sleep.

On a day excursion from the farm at Mona Vale the travellers called at a slab-sided building next to a gully full of luxurious vegetation:

The ground sloped down gently from the house to the little silvery creek that danced and sparkled along the bottom of the gully; whilst on the other side of the stream enormous rocks, grey with lichens or green with dank and slimy mosses, towered up in vast tiers one above another… Ferns and palms of numerous varieties

Aerial view of Mona Vale. Pittwater is in the background.

Mona Vale District Hospital overlooks Mona Vale Golf Course.

start up around… parasites, of strange, grotesque or monstrous shapes, batten upon the dead or fallen timber, or draw life from the juices of living trees; whilst shrubs and plants of the most varied and beauteous foliage are bound up and interlaced together by an infinity of creeping plants, some of vast proportions hanging and twisting amongst the tree tops like fabled serpents…

The owners of the house:

Were an ancient and a primeval couple, the man still hale and hearty – so much so that he started off to his work of felling and splitting almost immediately after our arrival. The dame, however, was somewhat the worse for wear, and being one of those characters peculiar to the Australian bush that – I had almost said happily – are now fast dying out, is perhaps worthy of a line or two of description. A countenance, pinched and shrivelled with old age, but bearing still the unmistakable marks of former days of misery, crime or degradation, and lighted up by dark piercing eyes almost as bright and fiery as those of youth, was framed round by an old-fashioned mob cap of soiled white.

Her stockingless feet were thrust into a pair of men's old boots cut down at the heel so as freely to admit the foot, and in these she hobbled over to the door to address me as I reached the house. "OH! ***** these ***** pains". The asterisks stand in the place of the expletives, which however elegant she herself may have deemed them, are scarce such as I feel inclined to place before eyes polite. I, of course, consoled with her and the pains.

"It's that ***** rhumatis, that's tuk the feet from under me. I never had such a ***** before. Until this winter, devil a smarter woman nor myself upon my ***** pins." Such was the style of her conversation, and she rather seemed to pride herself upon the variety and the originality of the foul expressions made use of. [The woman had heard de Boos was carrying a flask of spirits, and] something like the following colloquy ensued, though I omit the expletive asterisks, lest the compositor's supply of them should fail. "Well, young man,"… said she, "is it ye as carries the bottle?" she asked. I confessed that this was my part of the business. "Shure, then, my blessing on ye this very morning. Come in, come in; and let's taste!" she ejaculated. This threw me completely aback. I carried the flask, certainly; but it had been left behind, rolled up in my swag, and so I told her. "And what ——-," I leave the reader to imagine any possible number of asterisks here – "brought ye here? Don't ye know that the liquor's the life of the ould; and ye come with ne'er a drop?" I humbly told the old lady that our call had been purely accidental, and that, had we known beforehand that we should have made this visit, we certainly would not have come without the bottle. This somewhat mollified the old lady. "Well, well!" she answered, "Ye'll give us a call to-morrow, and don't forget the bottle. Sure you may shoot as many wallobi as ye like here." I thanked her, promised the bottle, and told her I would call going home. "Do! Do !" she said, "and then ye'll know the way back. But don't bring less nor a bottle. I wouldn't chate my mouth with anything under that." And at the very thought of liquor, the black, snake-like eyes of the old dame sparkled and glistened in such a way as to make me nervously anxious to clear out.

That evening, out on another 'Wallabi' shoot, de Boos spied a movement, fired, and shot one of the bull calves belonging to the owners of the slab hut. De Boos, fearing 'the tongue of that ancient dame' agreed with Tom who suggested

we must clear out. They've heard the shot… and by the dodging about of the lights at the house you may depend upon it some of them will be soon down here. If it's the old woman – I didn't let him finish; the picture presented to my mind, already shattered by the event, was too frightful to contemplate… making a detour through the bush in order to avoid any attempt that might be made to cut off our retreat, we hastened on as fast as we could… (and) the three miles that separated us from Mona Vale were soon got over. Arrived, we found a plentiful supper awaiting us.

Filled with good food, and tired after the day's exertions, de Boos retired but:

I will not pretend to say that my sleep was dreamless that night. Irate cows demanded their slaughtered calves at my hands, haunted my rest, gradually, as they waxed more and more wroth, assuming the form of the ancient dame at the farm;

whilst, as I tried to fly, ill-conducted wallabi stood in my path... "taking a sight" (at me). Only with the first cock-crow did these visions of the night pass away, and though I had been tumbling above and restless "grunting" as Tom observed, "like a pig in fits", I yet turned out fresh and ready for work with the first dawn.

Leaving Mona Vale by Barrenjoey Road, drive up the hill and turn right onto Hillcrest Avenue leading to Mona Vale Headland Reserve. Well worth the detour for the view across Bongin Bongin Bay towards Mona Vale, Mona Vale Beach and Warriewood Beach. Bongin Bongin, the original name of Mona Vale, were the words Aborigines used to articulate the sound of muskets going off.

Adolph Albers

Returning to Barrenjoey Road, as you continue north and glance across to the headland on the right you may spot some medieval battlements amongst the houses on the headland. This is Bungan Castle, built by Adolph Albers. Albers, a German migrant who arrived in Sydney in 1880 aged 14, was apprenticed to a Sydney art dealer then went into business on his own and represented more than 60 Australian artists over the years, many of them the best known artists of the day such as Sydney Long, Arthur Streeton and John Longstaff. On a journey to Pittwater in 1918 the cliff of Bungan Head caught Albers' eye and he decided it would be just the spot to build a house to resemble the medieval fortresses perched on rocky crags on the Rhine he remembered from his youth in Germany. The following year Albers bartered a Sydney Long painting 'The Westwind' for the headland with the landowner of the site, Alfred Yewen, and commenced

Bungan Castle in the centre of Bungan Head.

construction of his 'castle' from rock quarried close by.

The story goes that Albers would invite his friends to the site for a weekend party, then set them to work on the house from plans drawn in the sand on nearby Bungan Beach. As a result the house, though comfortable inside, is rather roughly built in a mixture of Gothic, Norman and Saxon styles. Albers filled the house with his lifetime's collection of works of art, antiquities and bric-a-brac, which he was always pleased to show to visitors, including the historian, Charles McDonald. The 'Baron' (as Albers was now known) showed McDonald a bugle which he claimed was used by Robin Hood in Sherwood Forest. Though McDonald thought 'It looked remarkably similar to the one I myself had played as a boy in a Cadet's Bugle Band! Good manners forced me to refrain from mentioning this fact'.

Albers retired in 1944 and lived at the house until he died in 1959. Though the castle remains, much of the original grounds have since been sub-divided and built on.

Bungan Beach

Bungan Beach is never crowded even on the hottest summer days because it is only accessible by a steep track at the northern end off Bungan Head Road. So unpatronised was the beach that it didn't have its own Life Saving Club until 1953. The Club's first shelter was a discarded Caterpillar tractor case.

Above: Aerial view of Bungan. Travellers heading north for the first time are unaware of the existence of the beach because it's out of sight of Barrenjoey Road. Left page: Bungan Beach and Head.

Pittwater

Aerial view of Pittwater. The estuary of McCarr's Creek is in the foreground, and Scotland Island is at the centre of picture.

Pittwater

As de Boos and his gang trekked north towards Palm Beach, the road passed 'Creel Bay' where

> … we had before us as pretty a marine picture as ever painter sketched… the clear smooth waters of Creel glistened in the sun, as the gentle breeze swept over its face and slightly ruffled its surface… Out on the waters of the bay, floated a smart little cutter… Behind her again stretched out the waters of the bay until they encountered the ranges of the other side, which coming down in many a ridge and gully, and forming many a deep indentation of projecting point, gave a gorgeous variety of tints and lights to a background that under a less brilliant sun or less pure atmosphere would have been sombre and monotonous.

Early history

Creel Bay or 'Careel Bay' to give it its proper name, is on Pittwater, a beautiful expanse of water about 10 kilometres long and an average of two kilometres wide stretching from Newport to a line between West Head and Palm Beach. Governor Phillip was the first white man to describe the district and it has enchanted visitors ever since. In his despatch to Lord Sydney on 15th May 1788 Phillip related how on

> The 2d of March I went with a long-boat and cutter to examine the broken land mentioned by Captain Cook, about eight miles to the northward of Port Jackson. We slept in the boat that night within a rocky point, in the north-west part of the bay (which is very extensive) as the native, tho' very friendly, appeared to be numerous…

Phillip described the branches off Broken Bay of the openings of the Hawkesbury River and Cowan Creek, then went on to tell Sydney that

> Here the land is much higher than at Port Jackson, more rocky, and equally covered with timber, large trees growing on the summits of mountains that appear to be accessible to birds only.

> Immediately round the headland that forms the southern entrance into the bay there is a third branch, which I think the finest piece of water I ever saw, and which I honoured with the name of Pitt Water. It is, as well as the southwest branch of sufficient extent to contain all the Navy of Great Britain,

According to the 1828 census there were at least 16 farms established around the shores of Pittwater. The flats usually had a ready supply of fresh water available in a creek or nearby spring and settlers used convict indentured labour to clear land, so were soon established as fishermen, boat builders, shingle cutters, orchardists, vegetable gardeners and timber-getters.

Pittwater was the haunt of escaped convicts in the early days who built their own rough huts from branches and bark and eked an existence from fishing and scavenging. Some even established themselves well enough to plant corn. According to the *Sydney Handbook* of 1867 a clergyman who 'penetrated the district' in recent years found 'many grown up people who had never visited the city' who were 'in a measure uncivilised'. According to Francis Myers in 1885 Pittwater

> was an outlaw's land (of)… escaped prisoners… Here they fished and planted, and made rude houses… and in places secured grants of land, which many of them still jealously hold. [The district was] only a quarter of a century ago… absolutely unsafe to travel without a strong police escort…

Wildflowers in the local bush.

But with more productive land available elsewhere, and also an easier style of living than scratching out an existence from subsistence farming, the landscape of Pittwater started to change. Maybanke Anderson writing in 1920:

> The bygone days of beautiful Pittwater, its early residents whose children are scattered far and wide, its farms and orchards, its ships and fisheries, are fading from the memory even of those who call it home, and it seems likely that it will soon be only a playground for the city whose youthful needs it toiled hard to supply.

Stokes Point and the boats of the Royal Sydney Yacht Squadron.

Bayview

If, when we'd left Mona Vale, we'd continued on Pittwater Road instead of taking Barrenjoey Road for Bungan, we'd have come to Bayview on Pittwater and been greeted by the sight of the forest of masts at Royal Prince Alfred Yacht Club. Bayview is named after Bayview House, built in 1882 near the shore of Crystal Bay by a local settler, John Collins. Collins ran the property as a guesthouse and had his own coach service to bring visitors from Manly.

Church Point

Pittwater Road follows the shore of Pittwater to Church Point. Church Point, first known as Chapel Point, is named after a little weatherboard Methodist church which used to stand on the hillside at the point. Before the church was built, Methodist laymen conducted open-air services under the trees at Bayview, inspiring a local land-owner, William Oliver, to offer the Methodist Church an acre on the point opposite Scotland Island for ten shillings on condition that a

Careel Bay.

A glimpse of Pittwater through the gum trees.

church be built there soon after. The church was constructed in 1872 for a cost of £60 and stood for 60 years until it was demolished in 1932. Some of the old headstones of the church cemetery still stand on the hillside, including many belonging to the Oliver family.

When Bayview Public School opened and in 1904 the *Patonga* became, according to the *Town and Country Journal* of 3rd August 1904 'the first and only school launch in Australia', picking up the 29 children living at Barrenjoey, Careel Bay, The Basin and other settlements and carrying them to the school and home again in the evening. Children from the settlements on the west side of Pittwater still catch a ferry to school to this day.

At Church Point there's a ferry wharf, one or two stores, and The Pasadena, a motel, restaurant and conference centre, which was established originally as a shop in the 1920s. A pleasant way to spend the day is to take the ferry from Church Point and hop off to explore Scotland Island, Morning Bay, Lovett Bay and Elvina Bay. The ferry, called the *Elvina* in a previous incarnation as the *Falcon*, was one of the craft used during the Second World War to tow all the boats from Pittwater to Berowra Waters. She also ferried soldiers to Mackerel Beach, who then marched to the fortifications at West Head.

Scotland Island

The ferry stops at wharves on both sides of Scotland Island, so it's possible to walk to the opposite side of the island and catch a later one back. Tennis Court Wharf and Bell Wharf have public phones so you can call for a water-taxi if by

Southern Pittwater. From left, Refuge Cove and Salt Pan Cove, the Pittwater shore at Newport, Mona Vale at the head of the bay and Bayview on the right.

The Royal Motor Yacht Club and Royal Prince Alfred Yacht Club at Newport.

chance you miss the last ferry, or alternatively you could thumb a lift from one of the locals who frequently cross to Church Point for supplies.

Scotland Island was known as 'Pitt Island' until 1810, when it was granted to Andrew Thompson who named it after his birthplace in Britain. Thompson was granted the 120 acre island by Macquarie on the 1st January 1810, the same day as Cheers and Gilbert received their grants at Manly.

Thompson, at the age of 16, was convicted of arson for setting fire to his master's haystack in a fit of temper and sentenced to 14 years transportation. He survived the atrocious conditions on the Second Fleet to arrive in Sydney in 1792, and became a policeman, receiving an absolute pardon in 1797. Thompson went on to become one of the great emancipist pioneers. He was Chief Constable of the Hawkesbury district, a post he held until 1808, built the first toll bridge at Windsor, established a brewery and hotel, and owned ships which he used for the Hawkesbury River trade. Thompson was commended by Governor Hunter for his actions in the 1806 Hawkesbury floods, when he saved 101 residents, plucking many from their rooftops in one of his boats. It was as a reward for further strenuous efforts in the Hawkesbury floods of 1809 that Macquarie granted Thompson the island

> Situate near the southern extremity of Pitt Water Bay... to be known by the name of Scotland Island, conditioned not to sell or alienate the same for a space of five years from the date hereof and to cultivate twenty two acres within the same period...

Thompson established a successful salt works on the Island, producing 200 lbs. of salt a week, and a shipbuilding yard, but he was already a sick man from his exertions during the 1809 floods and he died on 22nd October 1810. Macquarie wrote that his death 'affected Mrs Macquarie and myself deeply – for we both had a most sincere and affectionate esteem for our good and most lamented departed friend'. Thompson's was the first tombstone in the cemetery at St Matthews Church, Windsor, and his epitaph, composed by Macquarie, can be read to this day.

When the Island was offered for sale in the *Sydney Gazette* in 1812, the prospective purchaser was offered

> one hundred and twenty acres of good soil, extensive salt works, a good dwelling-house and stores, labourers' rooms... also a vessel of about ninety tons, partly built, still on the stocks.

The Island was sub-divided and sold off in 1906, except for the crown which was left as natural bushland and named 'Glasgow Park' (now renamed Elizabeth Park). It's a brisk walk to the 100 metre high wooded summit. These days the Island has a population of roughly 600 living in about 300 houses. Sixty per cent of them are permanently occupied and the rest are weekenders and holiday houses. The Island still relies on collected rainwater for its water supply, but was connected by electricity in 1965. All the residents had left their light switches turned on for the occasion and when the mains power switch was thrown at 10 o'clock at night the island lit up like a Christmas tree.

Morning Bay

The ferry's next stop is Hall's Wharf at Morning Bay on the west side of Pittwater. Most non-residents who alight here are going to the Youth Hostel ten minutes walk away on a track that winds uphill through the forest. The hostel is open to members of the Youth Hostels Association or to non-members at a slightly higher rate. Accommodating 32 people, the hostel is a former residence built in 1915 which was donated to the Association in 1966 by the then resident and owner Ibena Isles, a keen bush-walker.

Scotland Island.

Scotland Island from the ferry. Bell's Wharf is in the distance.

Southwest Pittwater with Church Point on the left, Scotland Island on the right and the estuary of McCarr's Creek in the background.

A waterfall near the tidal limit of McCarr's Creek.

Upper Gledhill Falls on McCarr's Creek were named after Percy Gledhill.

Lovett Bay

On leaving Hall's Wharf the ferry chugs across the smooth waters of Pittwater for the short journey to Lovett Bay. When the 35,300 acres of Ku-ring-gai Chase National Park were set aside in 1894, most of the park was an inaccessible wilderness. The section of the Park along the west shore of Pittwater was easy to get to by boat, so the Park trustees set about improving access to the bush. Four men were employed at six shillings a day in April 1898 to clear the tracks to 'The Lookout', the 'Flat Rock' and the waterfall at the head of Lovett Bay. The stone signs near the ferry wharf chiselled with '1895' and 'Lovett Bay' date to this time, as does the Aboriginal face carved into the rockface behind the beach. The track on the way up to the Flat Rock passes the gravestone of Frederick Oliver, son of William, who died in 1867. William Oliver, owner of 70 acres on the peninsula between Lovett Bay and Elvina Bay, built a house there called 'Ventnor' and had an orange grove on land cleared between the bays.

Some houses at Lovett Bay are modest week-enders, others are quite substantial, such as the 'Red House' built of stone on Rocky Point for 'Signor Stefani', an English artist-musician whose original name was Stephens. Other well-known residents were the actor and movie star Chips Rafferty who owned a holiday house at Lovett Bay and the poet Dorothea Mackellar (1885-1968) who used to stay in the 1920s house 'Tarrangaua'. Mackellar was recalled by the journalist Di Morrissey as 'a rarely glimpsed figure in black who smiled at you vaguely'. The writer George Farwell also lived at Lovett Bay. One day he set off with his children for Sydney to visit his publisher and arrived home without them. He'd completely forgotten he'd taken them with him.

The west shore of Pittwater with from left foreground, Lovett Bay, Rocky Point, and Elvina Bay.

The entry to Cicada Glen.

Elvina Bay

The final call of the ferry on the circuit before it returns to Church Point is at Elvina Bay, just 10 minutes walk away, so if you've alighted at Lovett Bay and have toured the district you can pick up the next ferry at Elvina Wharf.

McCarr's Creek Road

Pittwater Road finishes at Church Point then continues as McCarr's Creek Road into Ku-ring-gai Chase National Park. It is one of the most picturesque stretches of road in Sydney as it winds above the yachts and waterside homes along McCarr's Creek then plunges beneath the shade of the trees in the National Park. The creek that is its namesake cascades over several waterfalls and in spring the banks are lined with the buds of over ninety different wildflowers. Lumberjacks cut down trees on the banks of the creek in the 1920s and 1930s, some of which became telegraph poles on the roads of the Northern Beaches. Stands of casuarina trees still line the sides of the road. Called 'she-oaks' by the first settlers because the grain resembled that of the English oak, the wood was used for axe and tool handles, yokes and roof shingles. Don't miss 'Cicada Glen', a rainforest gully just off McCarr's Creek Road on the left next to the hairpin as the road enters the National Park. It's well worth taking twenty minutes to follow the creek up into a little lost world of creepers, moss covered rocks and rainforest.

Akuna Bay and Cottage Point

Ten minutes drive along McCarr's Creek Road from Church Point brings you to the tollbooth on West Head Road at the entry to the National Park. There's a small entry fee for cars, but no charge for the free maps of the Park offered by the attendant at the gate. Five hundred metres past the toll booth Liberator General San Martin Drive on the left leads to Akuna Bay and the road to Cottage Point. Boats are available for hire at Akuna Bay and Cottage Point, and there's a café and a restaurant overlooking the water at both places. Several picnic spots with benches and tables and wallabies to keep you company lead off General San Martin Drive.

West Head Road

West Head Road meanders and undulates through the bush to the spectacular lookout of West Head. There are a dozen or so tracks that lead off the road into the bush, and it is worth describing some of the more interesting ones. One of the best, which is the first on the right, is the Engravings Walking Track. As its name suggests, the track leads past some Aboriginal carvings to Elvina Bay. It then follows the old 1895 walking trail to the waterfall beyond Lovett Bay. The latter part is particularly pleasant through a rainforest type environment of ferns and cabbage-tree palms culminating at the waterfall. Backtracking the same way, opposite a Swiss style chalet the Flat Rock Track heads steeply up the hill past Frederick Oliver's grave to the lookout at Flat Rock. The track then winds round to rejoin the Elvina Track to take you back to the car.

Refuge Bay

A few kilometres further along West Head Road the Topham Track on the left leads to a bluff overlooking Refuge Bay. The Bay itself is only accessible by water, but is worth mentioning from a historical point of view. During the Second World

War, Broken Bay was off-limits to private craft and Refuge Bay was used as the secret training camp of 'Z Force' to practice for a raid on Japanese occupied Singapore Harbour. Using a wooden Japanese fishing boat that sailed to Australia just before Singapore fell, which was re-named the *Krait* for its new mission, Australian commandos entered Singapore under cover of darkness and planted limpet mines to sink many tons of Japanese shipping. The expedition returned safely to Australia with all hands and the *Krait* is now one of the floating exhibits at the Australian National Maritime Museum on Darling Harbour.

The Basin

Another one or two kilometres along West Head Road on the right a track leads to The Basin and there's a branch off it leading to Currawong and Mackerel Beach. The more usual approach to these three destinations is by the ferry which leaves from Snapperman Beach at Palm Beach, however as they are part of the Lambert Peninsular which leads to West Head they are described here.

Cabbage tree palms on McCarr's Creek Road.

The Basin really is a beautiful spot, 50 acres of lawn dotted with trees and a line of Norfolk Island pines along the shore backed by wooded hills that rise to a height of 150 metres. One imagines that if it had been on the Mediterranean the Greeks would have built a temple there. The Basin has a sandy beach with a view across Pittwater to Palm Beach and Barrenjoey headland, and at the 'Inner Basin' a large saltwater lagoon washed clean by the tides is made safe for swimming by a shark net stretched across the entrance. It's not a half-bad place to while away a Sunday,

The view of Brown's Bay on Pittwater from McCarr's Creek Road.

or if you wish to linger longer you can take a tent and provisions on the ferry and book a campsite at a very reasonable rate through the National Parks and Wildlife Service. There are shower blocks, a toilet and freshwater supply available.

The stretch of water leading into The Basin was named 'Coasters Retreat' because sailing vessels used to use it as an anchorage to take refuge from coastal storms. While waiting for the storm to subside sailors often replenished the ship's wood and water supplies. The surveyor J. Larmer mapped the district in 1831-1832 and produced a plan of 50 acres at 'The Basin' on 23rd October 1831, and in his field book of 1832 jotted down the names of 'West Head', 'Great Mackarel Beach' and 'Little Mackarel Beach'.

An early resident of the Basin was Peggy Morris, known by everyone who was acquainted with her as 'Sally', who had lived there since about 1870 in a hut close to the beach. Details of her early life are sketchy, but it is known she came from Parramatta and could remember the day on 7th December 1847 when Lady Fitzroy the Governor's wife, was thrown from her carriage in Parramatta Park and killed.

Sally's ramshackle hut had a stone floor and two rooms with walls papered with newspaper cuttings of yachts. She had chickens, some cows and a bull, and would swap hot food, coffee, fresh milk and eggs with visiting yachtsmen for a few shillings or for some beer and whisky. Some of the time Sally lived there on her own, and sometimes she was with a companion known as 'The Strongman'. In later years Sally cared for a succession of orphaned boys, five of whom lived out their childhood at The Basin.

Cottage Point. Coal and Candle Creek is on the left, and Cowan Creek meanders into the distance.

A family who had a long-time association with the area, the Gouldings, used to come to The Basin regularly for camping holidays. One Easter William Goulding borrowed a large tent from a friend for a big family gathering. They had a wonderful holiday and the day they were due to leave, before they broke camp, everyone went out fishing. The Gouldings' camp was on the south shore of Coasters Retreat opposite The Basin, and while they were away Sally's cows had swum across the lagoon channel to graze the grass and they returned to find the camp turned upside down, some of the salted fish hanging from the trees eaten, the tent ruined and 'doings' everywhere. William stormed off to confront Sally, a long time friend, about her rampaging cows, who replied 'Oh no Billy, my cows wouldn't do that, it must have been the bandicoots'.

One of the yachtsmen who used to visit The Basin was Fred Jackson. He was one of the founding members of the Royal Sydney Yacht Squadron and built 'Beechwood Cottage' at The Basin in 1882 as a holiday home. Sally was caretaker of the cottage when it wasn't in use.

The secretary of the Royal Prince Alfred Yacht Club recalled a holiday at the Basin in 1900.

> To celebrate the last Easter season of the nineteenth century the club arranged and carried out a General Camp at The Basin... On Thursday night most of the yachts put to sea with a wind light from the south and the sky with a little cloud, but later, the breeze hauling round west, the clouds broke up and the boats with their wind abeam danced along merrily as the moonbeams on the surrounding ocean, so that early on Good Friday morning quite a fleet of craft had dropped anchor... The presence of the yachts with a goodly display of parti-coloured bunting fluttering in the breeze enhanced the natural beauty of the scene by day, while at night the picture was delightful... [with] the full moon upon the still waters, the lights shining through the tiny round ports of the yachts [and] the artistic lantern decorations and fairy lights...

Sally Morris died at The Basin aged 84 in June 1921. In her memory members of the Royal Sydney Yacht Squadron, Royal Prince Alfred Yacht Club and Sydney Amateur Sailing Club erected a sundial on a stone pedestal by the beach near her hut inscribed with the words

> Erected by yachtsmen of Sydney in memory of Mrs Morris (Sally) who resided at this spot for over 50 years.

These days Sally's hut has gone (though the sundial still remains) but Beechwood Cottage is still there, currently in use as a National Parks and Wildlife Visitor Centre.

Currawong Beach

Next stop on the ferry after The Basin is Currawong Beach – it used to be known as Little Mackerel Beach but was re-named in 1977. In 1910 the beach and 48 acres on the flat were bought by Dr Bernard Stiles of Newtown and his wife, and they built a cottage called 'Midholme' there. Since 1950 Midholme and nine other cottages have been owned by the Labour Council of New South Wales. The cottages are available through the Labour Council for lettings, with slightly cheaper rates for union members. For your entertainment, besides the beach, and walks along the creek, there's a tennis court and a six-hole golf course.

Mackerel Beach

Last stop on the ferry before it heads back to Palm Beach is Mackerel Beach. The beach is also accessible by a steep track that climbs up and over the headland from Currawong Beach. Promoted by the real estate company selling

Liberator General San Martin Drive hugs the shore of Coal and Candle Creek.

Motor cruisers at Akuna Bay.

McCarr's Creek Road.

blocks there in 1920 as 'The Balmoral of Pittwater', a brochure described to prospective buyers

> the... picturesque lagoon... encompassed on the land side, by a buttress of noble hills, on the lower slopes of which a chain of knolls (every one an ideal site for a bungalow) leads sheer into fairyland... The gully... is overhung with palms and tree ferns and the usual tangle of semi-tropical foliage... Thence, amidst alternate sunshine and shadow tracks radiate in all directions through scenes of sylvan loveliness to innumerable points of interest... an arcadian farmstead nestles beneath the hills overhanging the adjacent beach and there on Little Mackerel amidst the gobble of the turkeys and the lowing of the cows future residents can safely rely upon Mrs Stiles for fresh milk, butter, eggs and poultry also for whatever groceries they stand in need.

These days Mackerel Beach is a village of 100 or so houses with streets of grass instead of bitumen between the homes, which sell for Balmoral type prices if they ever come up for sale. Houses on the slope on the south side are accessed by bridges over the creek. If you follow the creek into the gully there's still a pleasant shady wilderness 'overhung with... the usual tangle of semi-tropical foliage'.

West Head Lookout

Another six kilometres relaxing drive from The Basin Track brings you to the car park at West Head lookout on Commodore Heights. The Heights, which rise to nearly 200 metres, were named after Commodore Lambert, Captain of the Royal Navy ship *H.M.S. Challenger* which was in Australian waters between 1866 and 1870. A short walk brings you to a lookout on the headland with a quite superb view of Pittwater, Palm Beach and Broken Bay. If you tire of the views you can feed your chicken sandwich to the tame kookaburras. There's also a giant

The view of Barrenjoey from West Head Lookout.

Pocket of rainforest at the head of Refuge Bay.

Grass trees on the heights above Refuge Bay.

The Basin camping and picnic grounds. Coasters Retreat is on the right.

The beach at the Basin seen from the Pittwater side.

goanna who may give you a fright as he slithers across the crazy paving keeping an eye on his territory. He's never done anyone any harm though.

Six hundred and forty acres at West Head were granted to William Lawson in 1834 as a reward for the part he played blazing the first trail across the Blue Mountains in 1813. When Ku-ring-gai Chase National Park was proclaimed in 1894, this land was still in private ownership. It was offered to the Park trustees for £1 an acre in 1911, but was turned down. In 1929 a public road was opened out to West Head and the landowners proposed transforming the 640 acres into the 'Riviera Estate', producing a coloured brochure illustrating a country club, hotel, casino, recreation reserves and a golf course. The remainder of the land was to be sold for 2,500 house lots. However the scheme never got off the ground during the Depression.

In 1940, 50 acres were resumed at West Head and the headland transformed into 'West Fortress', with gun emplacements close to the waterline linked by a tram-line, observation posts, search light positions, an anti-submarine boom across to Barrenjoey Head and a military camp on the heights.

Resolute Beach

From West Head a steep track leads down after 15 minutes walk to West Head Beach. A climb back up the hill and a left turn at the track junction above the beach leads after a further 20 minute walk to Resolute Beach no doubt named after the schooner *Resolute*, which on 1st May 1877 according to the following day's *Sydney Morning Herald*, bound 'for Sydney from the Richmond, parted her chains this morning, and went ashore under West Head. She is bilged and full of water. The crew are safe'.

Currawong Beach.

Aerial view of Currawong Beach. Midholme Cottage is at the right of picture just below the tennis court.

Mackerel Beach, Pittwater, and Palm Beach seen from the Mackerel Track.

Rush hour at Mackerel Beach.

West Head Beach.

Rainforest scenery at the head of the creek at Mackerel Beach.

Resolute Beach.

Newport to Avalon

From left, Newport, Bilgola and Avalon Beaches. Pittwater on the left of picture.

Newport to Avalon

Sunrise at Newport.

Newport Surf Club.

After passing Bungan Beach, Barrenjoey Road skirts Bushrangers Hill then begins a long gentle descent to Newport Beach.

For many years Newport Beach was known as 'Farrell's Beach'. John Farrell was an Irishman who arrived in Sydney in 1813 on the convict transport *Fortune*, transported for seven years for 'possession of an illegal bank note'. Granted a ticket of leave, Farrell saved enough money to purchase 'a certain farm of land containing thirty acres or thereabouts, together with the house and all other buildings erected thereon' at an auction on 12th July 1822 for '36 pounds, 10 shillings'. The farm, on Pittwater just east of Taylor's Point, was called 'Belgooler'. In the 1830s and 1840s Farrell received grants of 150 acres at Newport, including most of the land near the beach.

On 30th December 1864 John Farrell's son, John Junior, was sentenced in Sydney to seven years hard labour for shooting the cows of James Therry at Mona Vale. These shenanigans didn't upset John Jnr's financial dealings because he became a successful landowner in Manly and by 1877 owned six sites on The Corso.

However, in 1861 when Charles de Boos and his friends came through, John Jnr was still at home in his farm at Farrell's Beach.

> In the centre of the picture stood the homestead, a long low slab building faced with weatherboards, and fronted by a verandah supported on rough bush posts that gave a kind of rude picturesque air to a building that would have otherwise passed as tame. It was perched on the crest of a small though sharp rise that started up from the bed of a deep and brawling creek which ran between where we stood and the house…

> [Crossing a bridge over the creek and surrounded by a pack of baying dogs] The loud challenge from these many canine throats [brought] forth the denizens of the farm, and from every conceivable corner, door, or window, forms protruded, or heads were seen, and men, women, and children seemed to start up into sight, where previously no sign of animal life had been visible… [They were welcomed by John Farrell Jnr] a fine strapping, fresh complexioned man, with a face the very personification of good humour, [who said] "Come in to the house. I'm heartily glad to see you, and so will the old woman be". With that he led us over to the house, and we entered by the back door… in company with our host, three young kids [goats], five puppies, and about seven children.

Farrell prevailed on his guests to go fishing at the south end of the beach on 'a flat ridge of rock running out very nearly a quarter of a mile, the whole of which is bare at low water', which they did, and very nearly got cut off by the tide and returned to the house soaking wet.

In the evening after they'd eaten, Farrell told de Boos about the origin of the name of 'Bushranger's Hill'. It had earlier been known as 'Casey's Hill' after an escaped convict of that name who, as Farrell explained to de Boos, used to rob farmhouses of food and clothes

> Along the Parramatta River on one side, and the Hawkesbury on the other. He used to come up [on the headland] after his expeditions, and lay by a bit, because he could see all around him for miles, if anyone was in pursuit of him… He was shot at last by a blackfellow – Black Bowen as we used to call him – one of the finest darkies I ever met with… [who often turned out in] an old dress coat of mine, a

regular swallow tail, that I had given him, and in which he would turn out as proudly as any swell in the land, although he hadn't another stitch on him.

That night recounted de Boos:

> I slept calmly and placidly... when towards the midnight hour, my slumbers were disturbed by a terrible outcry proceeding from Tom's chamber. I started up in bed, and heard the words "murder", "don't"... followed by what I imagined to be an attempt to say prayers that he didn't remember. I of course, jumped out of bed and ran at once to the rescue... [and on striking a match]

> There was Tom sitting up in bed, his face wearing the appearance of mortal agony, his hands before him as if to protect him, and jabbering away at such butt-ends of prayers as happened to come into his head. Standing on the bed, and immediately before him was a large goat which was playfully butting his horns against Tom's outstretched hands, causing him to shriek out at every touch. With the light, however, 'Tom's unbalanced mind regained its equipoise, and staring first with stupid astonishment at the goat for a few seconds, he gave it a lick of the head with his fist that knocked it off the perch it had assumed. Then, turning to me with a voice still trembling with agitation, he said , "Eh, Charlie, lad, I thought it was the devil". He had been wakened, he said, by a great big hairy thing trying to lay down beside him, and putting out his hands, they had encountered the horns, then the hoofs had made themselves felt as the animal stood on him, and when he sat up, all he could see was two great eyes as big as saucers flaming at him, whilst the horns were poked into his face. His thoughts had at once revered to the Father of Evil... and, his fears led him to believe that he was wanted... Farrell, who had joined us, now explained that the animal, which was one of a large herd of goats that he kept about the place, had, when a kid, been made a pet by the children, and that even now that it had grown to [full size] in the habit of sneaking into the house when it got the chance, and of getting into bed with the children or anybody else that it could get to...

Not wishing to stay longer as Farrell was pressing them to go on another

Barrenjoey Road at Newport.

Stormy day at Little Reef at the south end of Newport Beach. The Reef is exposed at low tide.

Newport from the rocks on the headland north of the beach.

fishing expedition on the reef that night:

> We took leave of our host and his numerous family of children, dogs and goats – with a full sense of the kindliness and heartiness with which our arrival had been welcomed, and of the hospitality that had pressed a longer stay.

John Jnr transferred his Newport farms to his son Johnny (the third) in 1881. Johnny, among other things, worked as a contractor for the Roads Department and built the first bridges on Pittwater Road over Queenscliff Lagoon and Narrabeen Lakes. He died aged 80 on 21st July 1933 after spending the day riding around the hills at the back of Newport on his horse. The old farmhouse described by de Boos stood until after the Second World War and was then, sadly, demolished.

Pittwater Road

Newport's development as a town took place because it was the shortest distance from Manly to the waterways of Pittwater and the Hawkesbury. This development was dependant on access via Pittwater Road and the provision of transport along it. The first exploratory journeys from Manly were undertaken to reach Pittwater to search for farming land in the vicinity of Broken Bay.

Though there were pioneer settlers who established farms north of Manly and at Pittwater, access to the district remained difficult, with no accomodation for travellers and supplies had to be carried.

Charles Jeannerett

So Pittwater and the Northern Beaches remained a remote seldom visited destination in the years to come. Land on the Pittwater side of Newport belonged to the descendants of William Wentworth (of Vaucluse House fame) and these estates were frozen and not allowed to be built on. They were part of the vast Basset Darley Estate, so called because after Captain Darley's death in 1864, his widow Katherine (nee Wentworth) married a squatter, William T. Bassett. This restriction on land sales was lifted by a special Act of Parliament in 1877 and land at Newport was bought by Charles Edward Jeannerett who ran a steamer service between Sydney and Parramatta. Between 1877 and 1879 Jeannerett built a hotel and pier on the Pittwater side of Newport, established a coach service to connect it with Manly and secured the mail contract to carry the post from the Hawkesbury to Manly from where it was taken on to Sydney by ferry. To service these activities he bought a small steamer, the *Florrie*, to carry the mail and passengers from Gosford and Broken Bay to the 'New Port' as he called his fledgling settlement.

In 1881 Queen Victoria's two eldest grandchildren Prince George (later George V) and Prince Albert travelled to Australia for a State visit, and Charles Jeannerett offered to entertain them for a day while they were in Sydney. The Princes mentioned the outing in a book they wrote on their travels 'The Cruise of *H.M.S. Bacchante* 1879-1882'. Leaving Government House, they travelled the short distance to catch the Manly ferry at Circular Quay.

> It was a beautiful morning, and having landed we got into two coach waggonettes that were waiting and drove away, past the boarding and lodging houses, their inmates all agog and aflutter to Newport on Pittwater... We drove in north-west direction, through level bush and a heavily wooded country. The road then ran towards the coast, and opened out upon a small lagoon called 'Dee Why' or 'Long Reef'.

They passed the *Collaroy* stuck fast on the beach just past Long Reef, and arrived at Newport where they 'found the steamer *Pelican* waiting for us with breakfast spread on the deck, for which we were now more than ready'. After cruising the Hawkesbury to Sackville, they then travelled on a carriage to Windsor

The view of the beach from Barrenjoey Road.

Sunny summer afternoon at Newport Beach.

The little wilderness of Crown of Newport Reserve.

The entry to Crown of Newport Reserve at Kanimbla Crescent.

and by special train back to Government House, arriving at 9.35 p.m. 'where we once more slept after a long and (thanks to Mr Jeannerett) a very enjoyable day'.

Newport

In the early 1880s the Boulton family owned the Newport Hotel and ran their own coach service to Manly. Harry Boulton used to drive the coach, and in the afternoon when the guests had finished their drinks and were back in their seats, the parrot on the verandah used to squawk, 'All aboard Harry'.

On 30th April 1888 the first Newport Public School opened in a tent. There, according to the *Sydney Mail* of 21st June 1890, 'A very interesting sight here for townspeople is the Public School... Here, under canvas, the Public School teacher instructs the young hopefuls in the mysteries of arithmetic, elementary physiology, & C'.

In the 1880s Surveyor Bishop drew up the outlines of the first streets of 'the Town of Newport'. They included Bishop Street after himself, and Gladstone Street and Beaconsfield Street after British Prime Ministers. Lord Beaconsfield was the title Disraeli assumed on his elevation to the peerage. Broad Queen's Parade named after the monarch was intended to be the town's main street and commercial centre.

The north end of Newport Beach. Bilgola Head is in the distance.

Tourists at Newport

By 21st May 1889 William Woolcott of the Sydney Tourist Bureau wrote:

> The number of passengers sent by this office over the Pittwater Road from Manly to Newport during the past two years is slightly in excess of 2,000 and the traffic shows an increase of between 50 and 75 per cent per annum.

Aerial view of Newport Beach. Bungan Head is in the foreground.

Though tourists could often also expect a little exercise on the way. According to a report in the *Sydney Mail* on 21st June 1890, on the journey north from Manly:

> When coaches with a heavy load encountered stiff hills, the passengers were obliged to make the gradient on foot, the stretch, however, does one good, besides relieving the horses.

But far exceeding the number of tourists travelling by road were those that came by sea. In the 1890s day trips to Newport were organised carrying up to 1200 passengers on large chartered steamers sailing from Sydney through the heads and via Broken Bay to the wharf on the Pittwater side of Newport. Sometimes there were running battles centred on the Newport Hotel when groups of larrikins from the Sydney gangs or 'pushes' caught the steamer for what they considered a productive day out, vandalising property and having a good brawl.

Newport by bus

The first motor omnibuses on the Manly to Newport run entered service in 1906. When the first two buses left Manly on their inaugural journey a huge crowd gathered to send them off outside the Pier Hotel near the wharf. Flags were flying and floral arches spanned the road. The buses of 'The Manly – Pittwater Omnibus Company Ltd' had seats for 16 passengers of dark green leather, a 22 horse power Aster engine with each cylinder separately cast which drove the vehicle at a top speed of 30 m.p.h. on wooden artillery carriage wheels shod with solid rubber tyres. The buses, which were chain-driven, completed the 17 kilometre journey in 49 minutes, a saving of 40 minutes over the horse drawn carriage which took an hour and a half. The first passengers included three M.P's, the Mayor of Manly, and Monsieur Houreaux, proprietor of the Rock Lily Tavern. However passengers found that they not only had to dismount for exercise, but were also expected to push if the bus expired on the way up Bushrangers Hill. That is if they got to their destination at all, because the bus frequently broke down completely. The buses were withdrawn after a short time because of insufficient patronage, to re-appear again – this time for good – in 1911.

The first telephone exchange opened at Newport in March 1914 with three subscribers, including the Newport Hotel. But this, as everything else, was on the Pittwater side. A map of 1924 illustrates the beach side of Newport as still all farms and the 'Town of Newport' on either side of Queens Parade. It wasn't until 12th November 1928 that a post and telephone office opened next to Barrenjoey Road on the beach side. Various names were bandied about for the new office, including 'Wongola', 'Karloo Beach' and 'Myola Beach' before someone hit on 'Newport Beach'. 'Farrell's Beach' apparently didn't get a mention, even though Johnny Farrell the third was at that time still alive and living on his Newport property.

Newport Surf Club

Newport Beach Surf Life Saving Club was one of the first in Australia, founded in 1911. In those days 70% of the ratepayers of Warringah, including Newport, were non-resident and many of the houses were weekenders. There weren't enough local surf lifesavers to patrol the beach during holidays, and their numbers were supplemented by outsiders, including some hardy souls who used to cycle up for the day from Mosman. The Club was one of the first in Australia to have lady members, but the Surf Life Saving Association was a men only organisation so the Newport Ladies' Surf Club was formed. At the first surf carnivals there were no trailers to bring the surf life-saving boats by road so

The town centre at Newport Beach.

A southerly buster blowing in. Seen from the walk from Attunga Road to Attunga Reserve.

A playground in the bush on Bilgola Plateau.

Bilgola from the lookout on Bilgola Head.

other clubs used to row to Newport for the occasion, including Bondi, whose team would row all the way to Newport then back again after a day's racing. The present clubhouse dates to 1933.

Newport in wartime

During the war there was a real expectation that if the Japanese landed they would invade Sydney via Broken Bay. In the years leading up to the war Japanese 'tourists' and embassy staff used to 'picnic' on the shores of Berowra and the Hawkesbury and energetically make 'sketches' of the surrounding scenery. To counter this threat an anti-tank ditch was dug across the peninsula between Bungan Beach and Pittwater spanned by a wooden bridge on Pittwater Road built in such a way that if a single pin was knocked out the bridge collapsed into the ditch.

The peninsula was considered indefensible and in the event of an attack it was intended to immediately evacuate all soldiers and civilians north of Bungan and the first line of defence would be at the tank trap. Newport was the first beach north of Manly with no barbed wire entanglements, so servicemen used to come there to swim. Children carried bags to school containing dried fruit, first aid kits and other essentials and practiced marching down to the wharf which was their expected route of evacuation. The wharf was mined so that once an evacuation was completed it could be blown up. All the boats from the Royal Prince Alfred Yacht Club and the Royal Motor Yacht Club were towed to Berowra Waters, dragged on land and camouflaged with hessian sheets, except for a few which were pressed into service for coastal patrol duties in Australia and the Pacific islands.

Sightseeing

The crown of Bushrangers Hill is the best place for a view of the Newport area. An ill-defined track leads through the bush opposite 26 Bungan Head Road to the top of the hill.

On the other side of the hill, Queens Parade East terminates in a lookout on the edge of the cliff. There's a view down onto Little Reef, where de Boos got a soaking. When there's a swell running quite a crowd gathers up here to watch the pattern of cross-waves that forms as the surf rounds Little Reef on each side then crosses over as it heads for the rocks. There's even a house at the top that's named after the phenomenon. Down below on the left is Newport Rock Baths. Dolphins visit the reef regularly and in late 1985 there was a school of approximately 30 which spent two days off the pool surfing the waves and feeding.

Another enjoyable walk is the climb from Kanimbla Park to Crown of Newport Reserve. The track, starting at the concrete path next to 9 Howell Close, actually follows the slippery rocks of the creek bed past some cabbage tree palms to a small rainforest at the top. A less adventurous access to the park is by the track at the end of Monterey Road.

Bilgola

Continuing our journey north on Barrenjoey Road, pass Newport Beach then swing around the headland and take the first road on the right called The Serpentine which winds down to Bilgola. The settlement sits at the base of a semi-tropical sheltered gully clothed in stands of cabbage tree palms.

When James Meehan surveyed the district in 1814 he named it 'Belgoula' which was Aboriginal for 'swirling waters'. Then a local grazier, Mr R. Henderson, who sold his farm on the Pittwater side to John Farrell, called it in the 1820s

'Belgooler'. On the 1904 map of shire boundaries it was called 'Bulgola' and sometime over the next 20 years the 'u' officially became an 'i'. The beach was in the past also known as 'Mad Mick's Hollow' and 'Cranky Alice's Beach' after two elderly early residents who berated any children who happened to pass by.

The first 'Bilgola House' was built above the beach by the politician the Right Honourable William Dalley in about 1870. Dalley (1831-1888) earned the distinction of being the first Australian to become a Privy Councillor. He was one time Attorney General and as Acting Premier of New South Wales was responsible for sending N.S.W. troops to the Sudan in 1885. His house at Bilgola had three large urns in the garden, one bearing an effigy of himself, and the others of Sir Henry Parkes and Sir James Robertson. William's son, John Bede Dalley (1876-1935) also lived at Bilgola and was a writer of satirical novels. He drowned while fishing off the rocks near the beach after being swept into the sea by a giant wave.

Writers must like the location because the author Morris West, who penned many novels including 'The Devil's Advocate' and 'The Salamander' lives here. So too did Thomas Keneally and he, possibly, had a room in his home there in mind when he wrote the novel 'Passenger' in which he mentions a house whose window was 'touched by the first diffused gold, of a sun that had travelled from Peru'. Also moved to prose was the author of a real estate brochure produced for

Bilgola Beach. Barrenjoey Road in the foreground.

Unusual rock formations on the headland at South Bilgola.

the sub-division and sale of 28 lots at Bilgola in 1922. The brochure, titled 'Bilgola, Gem of the Northern Beaches' described it as

> a charming spot on the ocean front, one mile beyond Newport… a little nest surrounded by undulating hilly country which protects it from westerly winds and the full force of southerly and north easterly gales… The road from Manly, which is only 13 miles, abounds with gorgeous scenery… The entrance to the property… forms an enchanting drive through tall and shady palms and ferns.

Bilgola House, which was replaced by a more substantial dwelling in about 1920, still exists near the car park at the beach. A storm in 1997 demolished part of the sandstone wall fronting the beach and destroyed half the plants in the lower part of the garden.

Bilgola Head

The Serpentine winds like a serpent through the pines behind the beach then leads to a lookout on Bilgola Head. This area was saved from development because 75 acres at Bilgola Head were made a Defence Reserve on 30th June 1884. It doesn't look as if it was ever fortified, but it's a good bastion from which to enjoy the views of Newport and Avalon. Charles de Boos would have come close to this way in 1861, when he and his companions rounded a curve in the road to be presented with a view of 'a broad swampy plain, or flat, which seemed to us to be inundated, for we could see the water sparkling and glistening in the sun over its whole face'. De Boos was reluctant to brave the swamps, but was urged on by Tom:

> This is the Priest's Flat, and there, where you see those shears erected, with the two tents alongside of them, is where they are boring for coal. We must go and report progress.

Reverend John Therry

The coal bore was an enterprise of the Reverend John Joseph Therry, who since coal had been discovered at Newcastle and Wollongong was convinced the seam ran in a continuous line beneath the coast. Therry, born at Cork in Ireland in 1791, arrived in Australia in 1820 on the convict transport *Janus* with the honour of being the first and 'only Roman Catholic priest for… the whole of the continent'; though for practical purposes his 'parish' covered the east coast from Melbourne to Brisbane. In the early days of the penal settlement practice of the Catholic faith wasn't encouraged as any gathering of Irish convicts, many of whom had been transported as rebels, was seen as a prelude to sedition, but Therry was warmly received by Macquarie who granted him the site for St Mary's Cathedral in Sydney and promised him 'all the land between Narrabeen Lakes and McCarr's Creek at Pittwater'. Therry was stripped of his post as a Catholic chaplain by Governor Darling, but reinstated by Governor Bourke who belatedly made good Macquarie's promise of land on the north shore. In August 1833 Bourke granted Therry 1200 acres on the peninsula between Pittwater and the Pacific Ocean at an annual rent of £9 8s 4d with a condition that it couldn't be sold for five years and that 85 acres must be placed under cultivation. With a further grant of 280 acres Therry received in 1837 his holdings covered almost the entire peninsula from Newport to Whale Beach including Avalon and Bilgola beaches. Including a grant of 100 acres Therry received at the present site of Cromer Golf Course in 1841 the priest owned property which in today's terms would be worth well in excess of a billion dollars.

Therry christened a cavern in the cliff north of Avalon 'St Michael's Cave', the

Bilgola Bends are framed by sub-tropical foliage.

The remains of an ancient temple have been exposed by the waves at Bilgola, but nobody knows who built it or where they came from.

Late afternoon at Bilgola Beach.

The view of Bilgola Beach from Attunga Reserve.

heights near Careel Head 'Mount Patrick' and the ground around Careel Bay 'Josephtown' where he intended a city would one day rise for which he had plans for a school, court house and cathedral. This project was to be financed by the extraction of coal which Therry was enthusiastically searching for, but when de Boos and his gang reached the earth boring rig they found 'the works… at a stand-still by the breakage of the apparatus', which was apparently a common occurrence, and de Boos reckoned that 'At no time have the men employed ever injured themselves by hard work' and recounted the story of 'an overseer that was employed [who] bolted with the month's pay of the men, and, not satisfied with that, took also the reverend father's horse…'.

Therry worked for years searching for coal at Avalon at an expense of thousands of pounds before finally giving up the project. Josephtown never got off the ground though a small weatherboard church the 'Barrenjoey Church' was built near the junction of Patrick and Therry Streets which was later, in 1918, moved to Narrabeen. Some of the men who worked on Therry's coal bore stayed in the district, lived in huts and grew fruit and vegetables, and when they died were buried in the cemetery at Careel Bay. Therry passed on in 1864, relegated by Bishop Polding to the post of parish priest of Balmain, and was buried in St Mary's, the cathedral he founded. The following year the cathedral burnt to the ground and the finance for the construction of a new cathedral was raised through the sale of Therry's land on the Northern Beaches which he had left to the Jesuit order.

Arthur Small

Avalon was such a long way north of Manly that it remained for many years native bushland populated by kangaroos. A typical picture, taken in 1906, shows just

Bilgola Beach. The quiet after the storm.

Gentle breakers running into the beach at Avalon at low tide.

Rock fossicking on Avalon rock shelf.

four houses at Avalon with the bush behind the beach traversed by the white band of the unsealed Barrenjoey Road lined by telegraph poles. Substantial land holdings in the district were held by Arthur Small, who wished to sub-divide and develop his estate but still retain the bush character of the area. Small's first task was to choose a name for the new settlement. Going to bed one night after discussing with his family a possible name, he woke up in the middle of the night shouting 'Avalon, Avalon, that's it! Avalon'. Avalon was the mythical paradise of Celtic mythology off the coast of Wales linked to the legend of King Arthur. It was also the title of a song of the 1920s, so possibly Small had the ditty on his mind on the night of his 'revelation'.

Small began land sales at 'Avalon' in 1921 of blocks of a minimum of 60 metres deep and 20 metres wide, imposing a covenant on the bill of sale preventing the unnecessary destruction of trees and banning the owner from further sub-division of the block. Lots were sold for £100 each, with two year's free membership of the local golf club and a 50% rebate on the purchase price if a house was erected within the first year.

Small's bungalow he built for himself and his family of four children still stands on Bellevue Avenue. Erected in 1920, Small named it 'Avalon' after the name of his new village. The house still carries its original nameplate, and has an east facing verandah which when it was built had a view of the beach. The view is now obscured by the surrounding angophora trees.

Avalon via Pittwater

An equally spectacular route to Avalon as by the beaches is to go there and return via Pittwater. Heading west along Queens Parade off Barrenjoey Road you soon reach Kalinya Street and the enormous Newport Arms Hotel. It is the fourth hotel on the site, the third burnt down in a spectacular fire in 1967. The terrace at the back is a good place to have a drink and a meal, enjoy the view over Pittwater, and maybe think about Watkin Tench, the first person to write about a journey this way. In June 1789 a party set off to explore Broken Bay, walking overland from Manly to meet the rest of the expedition on Pittwater who were travelling by boat around the coast. According to Tench:

> We arrived at the head of Pittwater before 11 o'clock, but no boat appeared which obliged us to walk round all the bays, woods and swamps between the head and entrance of this branch, [i.e. along the west shore of Pittwater to Palm Beach] by which [time] when we did join the boats we were exceedingly fatigued, the weather being rather warm, and each person having his knapsack and arms. This last part of our march increased the distance from 12 or 14 miles to about 25, in the course of which we had very high and steep hills to climb and many deep swamps to wade through.

At least there's a road along the east shore of Pittwater these days, but the circuitous route around the curves and hills is like a maze and so complicated that it requires a bit of direction. Leaving the Newport Arms, take Gladstone Street, King Street and Irrubel Road to join Prince Alfred Parade, which winds through the trees with a pretty view on the left of the moored yachts at Royal Prince Alfred Yacht Club and the Royal Motor Yacht Club. Prince Alfred Parade joins Loombah Street which climbs steeply past lush vegetation and tree ferns to Lower Plateau Road on Bilgola Plateau. Lower Plateau Road curves and undulates (this is a great ride if you come this way by motorbike) past desirable residences with well-tended gardens then joins Wandeen Road which plunges steeply through tall stands of eucalypts to Hudson Parade, which winds above

Surf carnival at Avalon.

Swimming class at Avalon Rock Pool.

Bangalley Head is the highest point on Sydney's Northern Beaches.

Left page: Looking south from Avalon. Avalon Golf Course is just above the south end of the beach.

Clareville on the Pittwater side of Avalon.

Palmgrove Park on Palmgrove Road Avalon.

Palms and ferns flank the entry to Hudson Park.

A tiny creek has cut a cleft in the rock in Hudson Park.

the shore of Pittwater past Long Beach and Clareville Beach. Sharks are known to inhabit Pittwater, so if you want a swim the netted enclosure on Paradise Beach off nearby Paradise Avenue is the safest bet. The long jetty on Taylors Road at the south end of Clareville belongs to the Navy and was established in December 1942 as a torpedo testing range. Disarmed torpedoes were fired at distance markers spaced out on Pittwater. The last torpedo was fired from the range on 31st October 1983.

Angophora Reserve

Leading off Hudson Parade, Hilltop Road terminates at Hudson Park, where a track leads through a magnificent stretch of virgin bush and forest to Angophora Reserve. The Reserve, opened by Sir Phillip Street on 19th March 1938, was named after a giant angophora tree, reputed to be the biggest in New South Wales. Sadly, the tree recently died, but its enormous trunk still stands near the entry to the reserve on The Circle. These two parks are a bit of a haven for ticks, so don't spare the insect repellant.

A split red angophora tree on a bush track in Hudson Park.

Continuing on our journey, Riverview Road contours around Stokes Point with a beautiful view across the channel of Pittwater to the bush-clad hills of Ku-ring-gai National Park.

Careel Bay

On the east side of Stokes Point continue on Cabarita Road and Patrick Street to Careel Bay, a sleepy little backwater dotted with the masts of the boats of the Royal Sydney Yacht Squadron. Did Therry really believe this could ever be a site of a major city? How could you build a cathedral if nobody came? The only monument to Therry these days is the nearby street carrying his name.

Stapleton Park

Wanawang Road leading off Patrick Street climbs the hill to Riviera Avenue which cuts through Stapleton Park, a delightful place to have a picnic and wander the bush to admire the 360° views of Avalon. Riviera Avenue drops steeply down the hill on the east side of Stapleton Park to return to Barrenjoey Road via Park Avenue and Kevin Avenue.

Careel Headland

Turn left on Barrenjoey Road, then third right into North Avalon Road and right at the end into Marine Parade. A short distance along Marine Parade on the left a short dirt road finishes at a reserve on the cliff top. Directly in front, a rough track used by fishermen leads down to the rocks. Five minutes walk along to the right leads to the fenced off entrance to Therry's St Michael's Cave. The cave used to be big enough to hold plays inside, but the roof has now collapsed. Back at the top of the cliff a vigorous fifteen minute walk up the grassy slope takes you into the bush of Careel Headland Reserve. Continuing north on the track leads after a further ten minutes to the very top of Bangalley Head, the highest cliff on the Northern Beaches with fantastic views towards our next two destinations, Whale Beach and Palm Beach. The track completes a small circuit through the bush on the headland then rejoins the track to the car park.

Whale Beach to Palm Beach

Barrenjoey Lighthouse and Palm Beach.

Whale Beach to Palm Beach

Dark Gully on Barrenjoey Road.

The story of development at Whale Beach is typical of the rest of the peninsula. Originally, no one wanted it. When the Napper Estate at Whale Beach was first sub-divided and put up for sale at the turn of the century not one block at Whale Beach sold. In the 1940s building blocks went for under £200, while these days it's not unusual to see completed homes sold for over $1 million.

Whale Beach is known, according to a recent newspaper article, as being home 'to the rich, famous and eccentric'. Some of these 'rich, famous and eccentric' people enthusiastically assist at the biggest fund raising event for the local surf club, the annual Miss Whale Beach Quest, open to all-comers. They sit at the judging, and 'rich, famous and eccentric' local ladies have also been glad to lend a hand recently with the addition of the 'Mr Whale Beach' contest. The first Miss Whale Beach, Louise 'Peach' Kyle, crowned in 1947, recalled 'being dragged into it by my father' in the days when the club was 'just a little shed'.

Palm Beach via Pittwater

There are two ways to drive to Palm Beach, each as picturesque in their own way as the other. The first is along Barrenjoey Road. Passing Hitchcock Park on the left and Careel Bay playing fields, the road passes close to Careel Bay before making a sharp turn around Dark Gully Park. Before the road was built the track followed the high ground then descended into Dark Gully, Junius writing in 1861 when he came this way on horseback found that it was:

> only a rough track over a mountain, rugged with broken rocks and gnarled trees…
> The 'inclines'… are somewhat startling… the descent into what is termed 'Dark
> Gully' [like]… those represented by Dore in Dante's journey to Hades.

The road meanders below the heights of McKay Reserve and past the shops of Palm Beach village to Snapperman Beach, which has a public wharf serviced by ferries which travel to the secluded beaches on the west side of Pittwater and ply the waters of Broken Bay and the Hawkesbury. The Palm Beach Ferry Service runs an hourly service for the round trip to The Basin, Currawong Beach and Mackerel Beach and a thrice daily trip to Patonga, only eight kilometres away on the north shore of Broken Bay by water, but a 130 kilometre journey if you travel by car. The service also runs a scenic 60 kilometre tour of Broken Bay, Cowan Waters and the Hawkesbury, with a lunch-stop at Bobbin Head in Ku-ring-gai National Park. Another way to explore the waters of the Hawkesbury is to take 'Australia's Last Riverboat Postman', which departs from a wharf close to the Hawkesbury River Station on the northern railway line. The wharf can also be reached by car by taking the Mooney exit off the freeway just past the Hawkesbury River Bridge. The Riverboat Postman carries the mail and the daily needs of the settlements on the Hawkesbury including the milk and groceries. Some of the tours include a smorgasbord lunch, and there are also shorter coffee cruises which include a complementary Devonshire Tea.

Snapperman Beach was named after the fish of that species that a Chinaman, Ah Chuey, used to dry at the beach. The intrepid Charles de Boos described his encounter with the Chinaman when he passed this way in 1861.

A view looking north. Careel Bay is on the left, Whale Beach on the right, and Palm Beach at the end of the peninsula.

Christmas Day at Whale Beach.

Long before our arrival at the tents, if we had had any doubt with respect to the correctness of our surmise, our noses would have at once dispelled it; for the strong smell of the fish, cured a la Chinoise, that saluted our olfactories was so overpowering as to cause us to hesitate whether we should give them a wide berth by making a detour. As it happened, however, that we required to replenish our stock of tea and sugar, it became absolutely necessary that we should visit the tent…

[de Boos approached the fish store] in which were piled up heaps of snapper and large-sized bream, all cured and ready, for the Celestial consumption for which they had been prepared; and here we found the two Chinese master and man, who owned the location…

[as] soon as the drying season is over-when the sun is so far from the zenith as to have lost its power – the packing is commenced. No further trouble is taken in the packing, than to lay them in the barrels as closely as they can be got, and to press them down as hard can be done with the hands. They are then heaped up and forwarded to Sydney, to be distributed all over the interior wherever Chinese most do congregate. This season they had obtained about two hundred barrels of fish… [de Boos sat down to have tea with the Chinese and] They had pressed us very hard to try some of their fish, and they certainly had a string of very fine fat mullet hanging up in their private tent, no doubt as a special delicacy, but, neither of us could stand the odour, which nothing but long habit or absolute starvation could have overcome.

Maybanke Anderson also mentioned the Chinese.

The Chinamen were particularly partial to mutton fish [abalone] and in their spare time were often seen searching diligently for the oval shell clinging to the rocks… they must have carried them in thousands to their camp, for old residents talk of the great pile of mutton shells which was heaped up near their garden. These were sometimes carried away by the children to make edges or borders for their garden beds; but the heap never seemed smaller.

Past Snapperman Beach the road climbs the rise to Observation Point, where the Aborigines used to look out for fish shoals, then swings round two sharp bends to a drive that leads past Palm Beach Golf Course and through Governor Phillip Park to a carpark on the sandspit. Little motorboats can be rented at the nearby Seaplane Wharf or at weekends and holidays small catamarans are available for hire on Barrenjoey Beach. One of the founding members of Palm Beach Golf Club, established in 1924, was Mr S. H. Hammond and a cottage he owned was used for the original clubhouse. His daughter, Joan Hammond, learned to play golf there and became New South Wales' amateur golf champion. She gave up golf and, as Joan Sutherland, was the renowned opera singer. These days Dame Joan resides at Whale Beach. The course is open to the public on Mondays, Wednesdays and Fridays.

Palm Beach via Whale Beach

The alternative route to Palm Beach is via Whale Beach Road which turns off Barrenjoey Road opposite Hitchcock Park. The road climbs the hill below Careel Headland then winds for two or three kilometres on a picturesque leafy route to Whale Beach. The beach is accessible by Malo Road, where a short flight of steps takes you down to the south end of the beach near the rock pool, or by The Strand where there's a carpark, the surf club and a cafe.

Palm trees at the beach

Whale Beach Road climbs to Little Head then winds above a low cliff with glimpses through the trees on the right of the ocean and Palm Beach. The road then joins Florida Road which takes you past Wiltshire and Hordern Parks, filled with palm groves overlooking the southern end of Palm Beach. A track descends through Hordern Park beneath the shade of the palms next to the creek to Palm Beach. There's a rock swimming pool at this end of the beach.

This section of beach is still identified on maps with its original name of 'Cabbage Tree Boat Harbour'. Turning right off Florida Road into Ocean Place takes you down to Ocean Road on the beachfront where there are a few shops including a cafe and a newsagent.

Stunning views

If you have more time for sightseeing on leaving Whale Beach, turn into steep Surf Road then right into Bynya Road which ascends the ridge above Whale Beach. At 69 Bynya Road on the right is Jonah's Restaurant and accommodation, which has its own little swimming pool and a quite superb view from the terrace of Whale Beach. The Duke of Edinburgh, then Prince Phillip, signed the visitors' book when he came to the restaurant on a visit to Sydney during his bachelor days in the Navy. A local girl, Jane Priest, once caused a stir when she planted a kiss on the Duke's son, Prince Charles, at Palm Beach.

A little way further along Bynya Road, Cynthea Road on the left leads to lofty McKay Reserve. From a rock-shelf there's a beautiful view through the scribbly-gum trees of Careel Bay and Pittwater. Bynya Road joins Pacific Road at a 'T'

Boiling surf on the rock shelf just south of Whale Beach.

Norfolk Island pines at Whale Beach.

junction. Turn left then 200 metres along turn right into Mitchell Road. At the end on the left halfway down the drive leading to number six is a small Bible Garden on a terraced lawn with the best view of Palm Beach in the district. The garden is the inspiration of Gerald Robinson, who created it after visiting a Bible Garden at Bangor in Wales. Robinson filled the garden at Palm Beach with plants from the Holyland including tulips, lupins, cyclamen, hyacinths and statice. The Garden, which is open to the public, was bequeathed by Robinson in his will to a trust. Don't forget to drop a few coins into the collection box next to the drive 'As a thank-offering for this view… [for] the work of teaching in St David's Church Palm Beach'. Nearby Rock Bath Road is connected by a steep track down to Palm Beach Rock Baths.

Continue west (towards Pittwater) on Pacific Road which winds round and down to Palm Beach Road. Turn left on Ocean Road, which follows the beach then rounds the corner to Governor Phillip Park.

Palm Beach and Barrenjoey

In 1910 Warwick Armstrong wrote in the visitors' book at Barrenjoey Lighthouse

> I've seen the sea in many lands
> In may climes and places
> But Barrenjoey is the spot
> To bring on smiling faces

Palm Beach and its headland of Barrenjoey is a place that you only come to if you are going there. It's at the end of a peninsula so is the end of the road. There's nowhere else to go. The place seems to exude a kind of distracted other worldliness. Christopher Koch summed it up well in his novel 'The Doubleman' which finishes at Palm Beach. He wrote

> The Barrenjoey Peninsular is different from the rest of Sydney. A long, slender dragon basking in the Pacific to the north of the city, it basks in the illusion of a different latitude and a different time-zone…

Early history

Visitors to Sydney have been making the pilgrimage to Palm Beach ever since Phillip led the first expedition here in March 1788. Phillip travelled north from Sydney in a long boat and cutter and was the first to record the name of the headland which he christened 'Barrenjuee', apparently after an Aboriginal word for a 'young kangaroo'. The local natives were friendly and helpful; as they made their way up the coast on 2nd March Lieutenant Bradley recorded:

> as we passed the sandy bay next to the South Head of Broken Bay we were met by 3 canoes having one man and 5 women in them, they came alongside of our boat quite familiarly.

The first land grant in the area was in 1816 when Macquarie granted James Napper R.N. 400 acres at Palm Beach and Whale Beach. Napper had served as a surgeon on the brig *Kangaroo* which was used for carrying stores, troops and provisions between settlements in New South Wales. According to the deed documents the district was to be known as 'Larkfield' and was granted on condition that Napper 'clear and cultivate' 45 acres within five years. The Crown was to be permitted to build a road through the property if it wished and to have access to any timber for naval used if so required. Napper sold the land to Robert Campbell who in turn sold it to D'Arcy Wentworth. Wentworth bequeathed it to his daughter, Mrs Katherine Darley and it became part of the extensive Bassett Darley estates.

A view of Whale Beach from the ocean with Pittwater in the background.

Small breakers rolling in at Whale Beach.

First settlers

The first permanent European settler was Pat Flynn who tended a large vegetable garden just below Observation Point on the Pittwater side of Palm Beach and sold his produce to passing ships. Perhaps he was one of the men mentioned in the Australian Directory of 1832. A track had existed to Palm Beach since 1822 and the Directory mentioned:

> At 19$\frac{1}{4}$ miles [from North Harbour there is] Barrenjoey. A rocky peninsula extending east and west and joined to the mainland by a narrow isthmus of sand. This remarkable spot is inhabited by three old fishermen who supply the farmers of the Hawkesbury... They also ferry travellers across to Brisbane Waters.

The Directory went on to mention that the three fishermen lived in caves and passing travellers

> 'were horrified at the sight and smell of the fisherman's hut'.

The Customs Station

The Palm Beach district remained a sparsely settled wilderness inhabited by the odd fisherman or vegetable gardener until 1843 when the Customs Station was established on the sand spit just south of Barrenjoey Headland. A year previously, on 13th June 1842, John Farrell of Newport and his convict labourer James Toomey were working on the shore of Cowan Creek cutting timber for a Sydney coachmaker, when Toomey noticed some casks piled near the water's edge. Concealed in some nearby high grass were 29 puncheons of rum and hidden in a neighbouring gully were nearly a hundred casks of brandy. It transpired the spirits were a cargo of foreign rum shipped from Sydney ostensibly for Lombok in the Dutch East Indies, which had been unloaded in Broken Bay, then stashed in Cowan Creek with the intention of smuggling them back into Sydney. The spirits, valued at £3,000, were seized by the Water Police and impounded, and the merchants who had exported them forfeited bonds of over £1,000 lodged with Customs against the spirits subsequently being relanded in New South Wales.

This was the most blatant of many cases of smuggling that were known to be taking place in Brisbane Waters and it prompted the authorities to establish the permanent Customs Station at Barrenjoey. The Customs Officer had assistance to carry out his duties of coastal surveillance, placing channel marker buoys and water patrol and inspection, a typical return of annual expenses for the Station detailing the Custom Officer's salary of £250 (a generous stipend to ensure no temptation to graft), coxswain 2s 6d a day, 5 convict boatmen at 6d a day, 6 rations a day 1s 4d, two suits of clothing for five men at £2 each a total of £448. On the establishment of the Station one of the first instructions of Colonel Gibbs of the Customs Service was to 'Form a winding path up the south face of the mountain by clearing the bushes and making steps where required, to a flat space on the top near the western end, where a sentry box or watch hut is to be built'. The track was cut by the five convict boatmen.

Life settled into a routine for the Custom Officer or 'Coast Waiter' at the isolated outpost of Barrenjoey. As well as their daily duties there was a vegetable garden to attend to and the family needs, because the Coast Waiters brought their wives and children to live at the Station. Alexander Ross, Coast Waiter from 1854-1868, crafted several effigies of soldiers and mounted them at strategic points on the sand spit and headland to frighten off smugglers. They had painted white trousers, red coats, a sword and scabbard hanging at the side, a black moustache and were crowned with a black shako (infantry hat) decorated with a

Whale Beach and Palm Beach. Cape Three Points can be seen on the west shore of Pittwater opposite Palm Beach. Tiny Resolute Beach and West Head Beach are sheltered by the folds of the points.

Whale Beach with Whale Beach Road in the foreground. The clear run of water in front of the rocks indicates the presence of a strong rip.

145

A ferry approaching the wharf at Snapperman Beach.

Pittwater, with Sandy Beach and Sandy Point in the foreground, Lion Island in the distance.

magnificent plume. One of the 'soldiers' can be seen on the beach not far from the Customs Station in an 1876 painting of Palm Beach from the top of the headland by J. A. Halstead.

The Customs Station was tucked close in to the wall of the cliff face of Barrenjoey and Ross was concerned that a rock overhanging his residence that was settling by an inch a year could at any time fall, and he informed his superiors that he had sent his wife 'to a place of safety'. The colonial Clerk of Works allocated £30 to employ Mr Doyle, a quarryman, to purchase the necessary quantity of gunpowder to safely remove the rock by blasting. The pieces were used to build retaining walls around the Station cottages.

Albert Black was Coast Waiter for 22 years from 1868 until his death in 1890. His duties, for each of which he received a salary, included Coast Waiter, Telegraph Master, Post Master and an Assistant Inspector for the Fisheries Commission. The station was connected to the outside world when a telegraph line was laid in 1870. Black was the first Telegraph Station Master, and in August the following year also became the local Postmaster when the 'Barrenjuey Post Office' opened at the Station.

Black's son, also named Albert, was the first child to be baptised at the recently completed chapel at Church Point in 1872.

Black never hesitated to row out to any ship in distress, and when the schooner *Resolute* ran aground in a storm on the beach which now carries its name, it was Black who rowed across Pittwater to save the crew.

In the 1870s an average of 370 ships a year sailed through Broken Bay and up the Hawkesbury to Windsor, but the trade declined with the silting up of the river during the drought of the 1880s, and by the 1890s the railway had taken much of the river traffic. There was no need anymore for a Customs Station and it closed in 1903. The handsome stone buildings were periodically rented as holiday homes until being maliciously destroyed by fire in 1976.

Barrenjoey Lighthouse

Since the 1850s a warning light had been placed in the window of a hut erected on the headland in rough weather. Then in 1868 the 'Stewart Towers' were erected on the east and west side of the headland that each threw a light about three miles. They were named after Mr Robert Stewart, M.P. for East Sydney, who agitated for the erection of a permanent light on the headland. With the increasing volume of coastal traffic and shipping entering Broken Bay a more powerful, taller, single light was required and the authorities requested the Colonial Architect, James Barnet, to design one. Barnet was familiar with the site as he had designed new stone cottages at the Customs Station which were erected in 1862. Barrenjoey, with its matchless setting, was Barnet's favourite lighthouse of the many he designed, and he bestowed the honour of laying the foundation stone on his 21 year old daughter Rosa. The party for the foundation stone laying ceremony numbering 20 or so, including Barnet's wife and Rosa, left early in the morning from Circular Quay on the steam *Emu* for Manly, then travelled by coach to Pittwater (their passage on Narrabeen Lagoon was mentioned in an earlier chapter) where a boat was waiting to take them to the wharf at Barrenjoey Customs Station. There was great excitement as the ladies were hauled up the steep incline of the headland in a small wooden horse-drawn trolley used by the construction contractor, then the party gathered for the ceremony beneath construction cranes festooned with bunting for the occasion.

Norfolk Island Pines cast shadows onto the beach on a summer afternoon.

Mr Greville, another of the guests, presented Miss Barnet with a solid silver trowel and a mallet, which was his cue to burst into speech:

> Miss Barnet – I have the pleasure of presenting to you, on behalf of the contractor, this mallet and silver trowel, for the purpose of laying the foundation stone of the Barrenjoey Lighthouse. They are implements small and delicate enough for such fragile hands, but yet in those hands they will be instruments for initiating a noble work. With a few light touches of this pretty piece of metal and a few taps of the mallet you will lay the first stone of a tower which will be the guide and safeguard of many future voyages. Above the spot on which you stand there will arise a noble beacon – the silent sentinel of the storm-tossed mariner, the shining monitor, warning those who brave the perils of the deep to shun the more obdurate dangers of these callous rocks. It will be a light looked for and longed for on many a darksome night. It will be the star of hope to many a weather-beaten crew, and the saviour of many a storm-pressed ship. It is for you, Miss Barnet, to place the first stone of that tower – a task easy in itself, but noble in its association, and fitted well for a fair hand and a benevolent heart.

The speech completed and the foundation stone duly set in place, there followed a hearty round of applause. After lunch and the return passage of Pittwater, the guests embarked in the horse-drawn coaches for Manly and, according to the *Sydney Morning Herald* reporter on hand, 'the dreaded Narrabeen was crossed in safety', and the expedition returned to Circular Quay 'having spent a day's unalloyed enjoyment'.

All the materials for the construction of the lighthouse except the stone itself, which was quarried on site, was hauled up the escarpment on the trolley track. The lighthouse and lightkeeper's cottage were left in their natural honey-coloured sandstone finish and the top of the lighthouse tower ringed by a gun-metal bronze railing. Utzon, the Sydney Opera House architect, used to have a studio at Palm Beach and walk up to the headland and thought the assistant-keeper's cottage of undressed sandstone was his favourite building in Australia as each block was different 'They are all like original oil paintings'. The residences each have underground sandstone tanks holding 6,750 gallons of rainwater and kitchen sinks hollowed from a single block of sandstone.

The foundation stone for the lighthouse was laid on 15th April 1880 and the building completed 15 months later, the first kerosene powered fixed red light cutting the night sky on 1st August 1881.

The Mulhalls

The first lighthouse keeper was George Mulhall (born 1814) who had attended the light in the Stewart Towers. At that time the lighthouse keepers lived in cottages at the site of the present day Palm Beach Golf links and walked along the peninsula and up the hill by the Customs Station path to attend the lights. George was the son of convicts Patrick Mulhall, transported in 1805 for his part in the Wicklow Rebellion of 1798 and a Welsh convict, Rachel Griffith, transported in 1804. Patrick and Rachel lived together and had children 'man and wife in the sight of God' as there was no non-convict Catholic Priest in the colony to perform marriage ceremonies. They were belatedly officially married by Reverend John Therry at St Mary's Cathedral in Sydney in 1830 and George was married to his wife Mary, also by Therry at St Mary's, just five years later in 1835.

Patrick and Rachel lived on a farm of 50 acres of land granted to them by Macquarie at Wagstaff Point (then known as Mulhall's Point) Brisbane Waters. It's visible across the opening of Broken Bay from the top of the headland. The road to the public wharf is still called Mulhall Street.

Palm Beach looking towards Pittwater. In this scene Palm Beach Surf Club is on the right, and the Rock Pool on the left is emptied for repairs.

When the shadows of the pines reach the ocean at Palm Beach it's time to head home.

Looking along Palm Beach to Barrenjoey.

The beautiful view of Palm Beach from the Bible Garden on Mitchell Road.

The Bible Garden at Palm Beach has plants that occur in the Holyland.

George Mulhall died in June 1885 and was buried on the headland. By rummaging around in the bush just east of the lighthouse you can find his grave. A message on the memorial stone reads:

> All ye that come my grave to see
> Prepare in time to follow me.
> Repent at once without delay.
> For I in haste was called away.

A myth has persisted ever since that George was struck down and killed by a tremendous lightning bolt while he was out collecting firewood, but in fact he died peacefully in his bed following a stroke. When George took up the post of lighthouse keeper at the Stewart Towers he brought with him as assistant keeper his third son George Jnr. George Jnr then took over as first light keeper at Barrenjoey on the death of his father until he retired due to poor health in 1891. George Jnr *was* once struck down by lightning on the headland but survived with a badly burnt arm which from then onwards he kept bound in snake-skin as an insurance against further visits from the Almighty.

Until the road was built to Barrenjoey, all supplies came by steamer. The keepers grew their own vegetables, cabbages, cauliflowers, tomatoes, beans and melons, had peach and apricot trees in the cottage courtyards and had fresh eggs, meat and milk from the ducks, chickens, cows and goats they kept. The nearest hospital was at Manly, so most deliveries were home births. Altogether over 50 children were born at the lighthouse and Customs Station.

A scribbly gum in McKay Reserve.

Barrenjoey School

Although it was an isolated posting at Barrenjoey, it was never a lonely one, because there were sometimes three families at the lighthouse and three at the Customs Station. With so many children about of school age a decision was made to establish a school. Known as the Barrenjoey Provisional School, it was the first school north of Manly and opened in 1871 in a boatman's cottage at Chinaman's Beach (Snapperman Beach). By the following year there were 24 pupils attending, including eight who were from the Customs Station. A school at Palm Beach functioned haphazardly for 32 years until the *Patonga* school launch started her run and children from Barrenjoey transferred to Bayview School. Bill Warren, son of one of the assistant keepers at the lighthouse, once told of how he would trail logs in the boat's wake to 'slow down' the launch on the way to school.

Departure of the Lightkeepers

In 1932 the light at Barrenjoey lighthouse was converted from kerosene to automatic acetylene operation, increasing its power from 700 candle to 6,000 candles. That year a Commonwealth notice advised mariners 'The Lightkeepers have been withdrawn and the light is now unwatched. The telephone has been disconnected and [manual] signalling discontinued'. One of the duties of the lightkeepers had been to hoist signal flags on the flagstaff on the headland to warn seafarers of an approaching storm or heavy swell running in Broken Bay. The closing reference in the visitors' book stated the Lightkeepers had left the Station with their furniture and effects and 'no person was on the Station for the first time since the light was first established in 1868… a period of 64 years'. The lighthouse was converted to an electric powered 1,000 watt tungsten lamp in 1972 with an output of 75,000 candlepower and a geographical range of 26 nautical miles. The lightkeeper's cottages were neglected and soon became

A sphinx-like rock formation on the rocks between Palm Beach and Whale Beach.

derelict, but were restored by tenants, including Jervis Sparks, who wrote an informative history of the headland 'Tales from Barranjoey'.

Settlement of Palm Beach

Though there was plenty of activity in the early days at the Customs Station and Lighthouse, the rest of the peninsula remained virtually deserted. In 1912 when an auction of 88 newly sub-divided blocks took place, it was easier to bring prospective patrons by ferry from Newport to a wharf at Snapperman Beach than it was over the rough track along the peninsula. The real estate agents Raine and Horne advertised the land sale as the 'Barrenjoey Palm Beach Estate' the first known reference to Palm Beach and the name that was adopted for the suburb.

The road to Palm Beach was upgraded for cars in 1920, but even then people didn't flock to the district. There was no road on the beach side, the road next to Pittwater finished at the golf course. A 1925 photo of the Ocean Beach shows only half a dozen houses near the beach and three or four on the hill overlooking the southern end. One of them was built by the Hordern family of the famous city store, who owned land at Palm Beach. R. J. Hordern directed the planting of Norfolk Island Pines along the beachfront in 1914-1915. Hordern Park was once part of the family estate.

In October 1938 the 190 bus service was established from Wynyard to Palm Beach. The 40 kilometre route run by the double-deckers was the longest in metropolitan Sydney and takes an hour and a quarter traffic permitting. During the War it was thought the double-deckers may need to carry soldiers to the peninsula to repel a Japanese invasion, and they were painted in camouflage and the windows replaced by shutters. The buses on the 190 route were the last double-deckers operating in Sydney because the new long articulated buses of the Urban Transit Authority couldn't get round the Bilgola Bends. The double-deckers were withdrawn from service when the bends were widened in 1986.

A Frenchman at Barrenjoey

Charles de Boos walked along the crest of the sandspit towards Barrenjoey in 1861, and observed:

> two... persons standing on a high sandy ridge near the [Customs] house. One of these was Mr Ross, the Custom-house officer... but who was the other? He appeared to be a military officer, for he had the orthodox scarlet swallow-tail and infantry shako... Tom [who was already with Ross] shouted to us, and we took off our hats in salute. Mr Ross returned the compliment, but the red coated gentleman... [took no] notice of us.

> [de Boos met Ross and] Now, it struck me, that as we were to pass the evening here... at all events the ice should be broken between us and the military gentleman, who I regretted to find, did not come up to join us... [following Ross] back up the hill... A dozen or so paces brought us to the top of the sand hill, and there to my intense surprise and disgust, I found that Ross' military friend was nothing more than a painted log of wood... [when his friends burst out laughing] I could stand no more, so clubbing my [fowling] piece I rushed on the scarlet-coated deception and should most certainly have smashed it... if Ross had not thrown himself across my path and stayed my murderous hand.

> 'Don't hurt it', he said, 'For I had a good deal of trouble getting that piece of wood'. And here he showed me that it was almost the natural form of the wood that made the figure, one leg of the particular shape required forming the head, body and legs, and the arms being short boughs inserted into auger holes bored for the purpose... Out of respect to our host I contrived to calm my fluried spirits, although at every opportunity that offered, I shook my fist at the effigy, and once when Ross' back was

Tree ferns and cabbage tree palms in Hordern Park.

Palms in the sheltered gully overlooking the south end of Palm Beach.

153

Palm Beach Golf Course. Barrenjoey Beach and the seaplane wharf on Pittwater are on the left.

The majestic headland of Barrenjoey. Like a hammer-head shark about to pounce.

turned, with savage delight I knocked off the old black hat that covered its top…

De Boos and his friends were escorted by Ross to his cottage at the Customs Station.

> At the back of the cottage we were shown, with evident pride, the arrangements that had been made for supplying the station with water. These were effected by bringing the water of a beautifully clear and crystal spring, by means of long troughs from a dank, rocky gully in the mountain's side, whence it took its source, down to the back of the premises, and within easy reach of the domestics. This stream, which has never been known to fail, even in the dryest season, is said to be deliciously cold and refreshing in hot weather, and to have cooling properties almost equal to those of ice.
>
> Everywhere about the place, in the paved yards, the carefully kept paths in every direction, the painted and secure fences, the constantly repaired houses and the well tended gardens, are shown the marks of minute and ever watchful care, such as is seldom met with in the locations of the bush. All looks as neat, and as clean, and as pretty as if it was a dolls house, newly turned out of the toy-shop; and yet, close upon it tower up the rude bluff rocks of Barrenjuee, heaped one upon another in massive and Titanic tiers, until the eye gets giddy in following them. Here again, Ross's never tiring hand has been at work, and he has contrived to cut a very creditable pathway up the side of the mountain from the corner of his fencing to a gap that occurs between two of the hummocks on its summit. Here he has a rustic seat, guarded by a military dummy, counterpart of the one to whom I had been introduced on the hill below; and here, spy glass in hand, he takes notice of the numerous vessels that pass or that come into Broken Bay.

A yacht race off Barrenjoey.

The walk to the Lighthouse

From the Seaplane Wharf on Barrenjoey Beach, five minutes walk north on the beach takes you to the base of the headland. Just before the end of the beach is a track on the right that leads to the lighthouse. Near the start of the track a path leads up some steps on the right. This path, recently upgraded by the National Parks and Wildlife Service, is the original path cut by the convicts for the Customs officers to reach their lookout. It traverses the south escarpment of Barrenjoey, and comes out on the headland just below the lightkeepers' cottages. For the twenty minute walk to the top of the headland my recommendation would be take the customs trail on the way up and to return by the broad track leading directly west from the lighthouse. This second track was built to haul supplies up the hill to the lighthouse and lightkeepers' cottages by horse and cart. It's still paved in places with the original sandstone slabs.

The slopes and summit of Barrenjoey are still clothed in quite thick bush. In an 1881 photograph of Barrenjoey Head the vegetation looks much sparser than it does today because an old man who lived close to the beach used to graze a hundred goats there. As well as devouring much of the bush they ate all the rock lilies. The goats were shot by a local gun club in the 1930s. No kangaroo or wallaby has been seen on the headland since the late 1940s, though there were still koalas in the trees of Shark Point on the west side of Barrenjoey until 1967 when they all perished in a bushfire. There's still plenty of birdlife on the headland though and their twittering keeps you company as you ascend the hill and the occasional kookaburra, magpie or nankeen kestrel provides an interesting diversion as it flies overhead.

Ross' military dummy succumbed in a bush fire in 1912, but you can still enjoy the spectacle from the top described by de Boos, who found:

> truly it is a magnificent view that is spread out before me, as I recline in that seat on the summit of Barrenjuee, and smoke my pipe. Away to the left, I can see the

The paved track to the lighthouse resembles an ancient Roman Road.

mouth of the Hawkesbury, and can trace that river up a considerable distance until it is shut in by numerous woody headlands. Almost in front of it, lies Mount Elliott receiving its name from its very remarkable resemblance to a lion *couchant*, the emblem of the Elliotts. To the north of that again, and extending away to the right, is a long sandy beach, upon which the sea breaks in heavy and ceaseless rollers for nearly a mile from the shore. This beach stretches away right to the entrance of Brisbane Water, and forms one side of that entrance, the other being a pecked and pyramidal-looking hill, which looks grey and indistinct in the distance. More in the foreground, there stand Little Box Head, and from where I stand, the sea appears to break right across from this headland almost to Mt Elliott, and although there is a channel, constantly shifting, I cannot see it at so great a distance. From Little Box Head to the North Head of Broken Bay, a distance of six or seven miles, there is a constant succession of headlands and long sandy beaches, with here and there a bluff faced wall of rock with a long reef running out from it, as though Old Ocean had made some more savage attack than ordinary upon this particular spot and had shaved it down to the ordinary marine level. Here we sat and gazed and gazed, at each instant finding out something new, some mellow light, some deep shadow, until at last the setting sun threw his last crimson glow upon the western hills, and then the prospect began to fade gradually away; the more distant parts receding piecemeal from view, retreating behind the veil of haze that seemed to come down before them and to advance slowly, step by step as the twilight deepened into night. At the very same time, the wind came upon us cold and bleak, off the vast expanse of water, and with something like a longing for the snug parlour and the cheery fireside, we hurried down the hill to the cottage.

Lion Island

Mount Elliott, mentioned by de Boos, is the island in the middle of Broken Bay. Covering 8.9 hectares and rising to a height of 86 metres, it has never been inhabited and since 1933 has been a public reserve and wildlife refuge. In the late nineteenth century steamers used to take daytrippers there from Sydney for the day. The island was mentioned by Captain John Hunter, who during his survey of Broken Bay in August and September 1789 recorded that in the wide opening of the Bay was:

> A very high rocky island, of but small extent, its eastern end is very high and perpendicular... now called Mount Elliot, from it's similarity to the north end of Gibraltar Rock.

The island was named after General Elliott, a friend of Governor Phillip's, who defeated the French and Spanish fleets in two engagements at Gibraltar in 1781-1782. However, for over 100 years the rock has been known as 'Lion Island' because, as one traveller wrote in the 1880s:

> indeed it looks like a gigantic lion crouching at the entrance of the river... like a monster of the primitive world turned into stone.

And on that note, its time to head home, or as de Boos put it:

> Seeing that we were now at the extreme verge of the peninsula, and that no further advance could be made, it followed as a matter of necessity that we should counter-march, or, in bush parlance, take the back track.

The track to the lighthouse climbs the west side of Barrenjoey Headland.

The lighthouse and lightkeeper's cottages.

Lion Island, guarding the entrance to Broken Bay, is an uninhabited nature reserve.

Index

Numbers in italics refer to illustrations

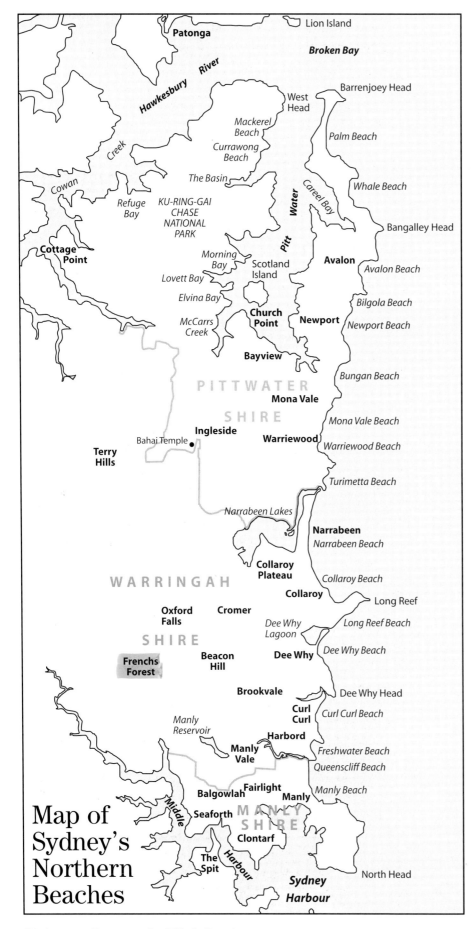

Map of Sydney's Northern Beaches

Back cover: Dawn surf at Whale Beach.

Bibliography

Anderson, Maybanke; *The story of Pittwater*, 1920.

Champion, Shelagh and George; *Manly, Warringah and Pittwater 1788-1850*, 1997.

Clark, L.A. *North of the Harbour: A brief history of transport to and on the North Shore*, 1946.

de Boos, Charles; *My Holiday*, a story of the journey from Manly to Barrenjoey from the 'Sydney Mail' starting 22nd June 1861 and continuing for the following consecutive 13 Saturday editions.

Fairfax, John; *Historic Roads round Sydney*, 1951.

Frenchs Forest Fonograph; Vol. 1, No. 1, 21 Oct 1917.

Gledhill, Percy; *Manly and Pittwater: its beauty and progress*, 1948.

Gordon, Gwen; *Harbord, Queenscliff and South Curl Curl 1788-1978*, 1978.

Hiking for Health: Explore Manly, Frenchs Forest and Warringah. Port Jackson and Manly Steamship Co, 1936.

Jennings, Guy; *The Newport Story 1788-1988.* 1987.

Lawrence, Joan; *Pittwater Paradise*, 1994.

McDonald, Charles; *Manly - Warringah: Stories of the Peninsular*, 1979.

McDonald, Charles; *Stories of the Peninsular, Manly - Warringah. A new collection from the 'Manly Daily'*, 1980.

McDonald, Charles and C. Henderson; *The Manly Warringah Story*, 1975.

Myers, Francis; *Beautiful Manly: Its approaches, surroundings, charms and history*, 1885.

Palm Beach Estate, Barrenjoey; Raine and Horne, 1912.

Retallack, Greg; *Geological excursion guide to the sea cliffs north of Sydney*, 1976.

Sharpe, Alan; *Pictorial Memories: Manly to Palm Beach*, 1983.

Sparks, Jervis; *Tales from Barrenjoey*, 1992.

Studios, E.B.; *Bilgola, Gem of the Northern Beaches*, c.1922.

Swancott, Charles; *Manly: 1788 to 1968*, 1968.

Vialoux, A; *Manly and Warringah Shire: An illustrated history of the town of Manly and guide to Warringah Shire*, 1922.